T0355668

WRITERS AND THEIR WORK

ISOBEL ARMSTRONG
General Editor

ALICE MUNRO

ALICE MUNRO

ALICE MUNRO

Ailsa Cox

Northcote House
in association with the
British Council

© Copyright 2004 by Ailsa Cox

First published in 2004 by Northcote House Publishers Ltd, Horndon, Tavistock,
Devon, PL19 9NQ, United Kingdom.
Tel: +44 (01822) 810066. Fax: +44 (01822) 810034.

British Library Cataloguing-in-Publication Data
A catalogue record for this book is available from the British Library

ISBN 0-7463-1127-3 hardcover
ISBN 0-7463-0992-9 paperback

Typeset by TW Typesetting, Plymouth, Devon
Printed and bound by CPI Group (UK) Ltd, Croydon, CR0 4YY

Contents

Biographical Outline

1931	Born 10 July, Wingham, in Huron County, south-western Ontario. Eldest of three children born to Anne and Robert Laidlaw. Mother an ex-school-teacher; father farms mink and fox, and, later, turkeys. Mixed Scots, Irish and English ancestry. On father's side, descended from James Hogg (1770–1835), author of *The Private Memoirs and Confessions of a Justified Sinner, Written by Himself*.
1943	Mother becomes ill with Parkinson's disease. Alice takes over household chores.
1949–51	Two-year scholarship to University of Western Ontario, studying English. Works part-time in public library. Publishes her first stories in the *Folio*, student literary magazine.
1951	Leaves university. Marries fellow student James Munro and moves to Vancouver. He works as executive for Eaton's department store. She works in public library. Sells first short story to Canadian Broadcasting Corporation.
1953–6	First daughter, Sheila, born. Sells story, 'A Basket of Strawberries', to *Mayfair* magazine. Stories accepted regularly for Canadian magazines and radio. Second baby daughter, Catherine, dies shortly after birth.
1957	Third daughter, Jenny, born.
1959	Mother dies. Writes 'The Peace of Utrecht'.
1963	Munro family moves to Victoria, British Columbia to start up a bookshop.
1966	Fourth daughter, Andrea, born.

1968	First collection published, *Dance of the Happy Shades*. Wins Governor General's Award.
1971	*Lives of Girls and Women* published. Wins Canadian Booksellers' Award.
1972–3	Marriage breaks up. Moves back to Ontario with Andrea and Jenny.
1974	*Something I've Been Meaning to Tell You* published. Writer in Residence, University of Western Ontario. CBC television adaptation of 'Baptizing' (*Lives of Girls and Women*). Daughter Jenny plays Del Jordan.
1976	Honorary doctorate, University of Western Ontario. Marries Gerald Fremlin, a geographer, also from Huron County, whom she first met at university. Father dies. Represented by American agent, Virginia Barber.
1977	'Royal Beatings' published in the *New Yorker*. Wins Canada-Australia Literary Prize.
1978	*Who Do You Think You Are?* published. Wins Governor General's Award. Retitled *The Beggar Maid* (shortlisted for Booker Prize, 1980). Screenplay, *1847: The Irish*, broadcast by CBC.
1979	Visits Australia. Robert Laidlaw's novel, *The McGregors: A Novel of an Ontario Pioneer Family* published posthumously.
1980	Writer in Residence, University of British Columbia, Vancouver, then at University of Queensland, Australia.
1981	Trip to China with group of Canadian writers.
1982	*The Moons of Jupiter* published. Book tour to Scandinavia. First academic conference on Munro, at University of Waterloo, Ontario.
1986	*The Progress of Love* published. Wins Governor General's Award. First recipient of Marian Engel award.
1990	*Friend of My Youth* published.
1991	*Friend of My Youth* wins Commonwealth Writers' Prize (Canada and Caribbean region). Receives Canada Council Molson Prize for lifetime contribu-

	tion to Canadian cultural life. Becomes a grand-mother.
1994	*Open Secrets* published. Wins W. H. Smith Award (1995).
1996	*Selected Stories* published.
1998	*The Love of a Good Woman* published. Wins US National Book Critics' Circle fiction prize (1999); Giller Prize (largest Canadian prize).
2001	Wins Rea Award for achievement in the short story form in North America and Canada. Sheila Munro's memoir, *Lives of Mothers and Daughters*, published. Publishes her fortieth *New Yorker* story ('Floating Bridge'). *Hateship, Friendship, Courtship, Loveship, Marriage* published.
2002	*Hateship, Friendship, Courtship, Loveship, Marriage* wins Commonwealth Writers' Prize (Canada and Caribbean region). Attends the opening of a public garden created in her honour in her hometown, Wingham, on her seventy-first birthday.

Abbreviations and References

By Alice Munro

BM	*The Beggar Maid* (Harmondsworth: Penguin, 1988)
DHS	*Dance of the Happy Shades* (London: Vintage, 2000)
EH	'Everything Here is Touchable and Mysterious', *Weekend Magazine, Toronto Star*, 5 November 1974
FMY	*Friend of My Youth* (London: Vintage, 1991)
HFC	*Hateship, Friendship, Courtship, Loveship, Marriage* (London: Chatto & Windus, 2001)
LGW	*Lives of Girls and Women* (Harmondsworth: Penguin, 1984)
MJ	*The Moons of Jupiter* (London: Vintage, 1997)
OS	*Open Secrets* (London: Vintage, 1995)
PL	*The Progress of Love* (London: Flamingo, 1988)
SBM	*Something I've Been Meaning to Tell You* (Harmondsworth: Penguin, 1987)
TLGW	*The Love of a Good Woman* (London: Vintage, 2000)
WR	'What is Real?', in How Stories Mean, ed. J. Metcalf and J. R. (Tim) Struthers (Erin, Ontario: Porcupine's Quill, 1993), 331–4

On Alice Munro

Tausky	Thomas E. Tausky, 'Biocritical Essay', in *The Alice Munro Papers: First Accession*, ed. Apollonia Steele and Jean F. Tener (Calgary: University of Calgary Press, 1986), x–xxiv
PR	Interview with Alice Munro by Jeanne McCulloch and Mona Simpson, *Paris Review*, 131 (Summer 1994), 227–64

Introduction

Alice Munro is one of the few living writers whose reputation stands on the short story. She has chosen to work almost entirely within this genre, condensing whole lifetimes into complex narrative structures where past and present, truth and fantasy, art and fiction, cross into one another. With ten books published her status now seems assured. In a career which first took off in the 1960s, she has gathered numerous literary prizes, including three Canadian Governor General's Awards. *The Beggar Maid* was on the 1980 Booker shortlist in Britain. Twenty years later *The Love of a Good Woman* carried off Canada's most lucrative prize, the Giller, and – unusually, for a non-American author – the US National Book Critics' Circle prize for fiction. Her most recent collection, *Hateship, Friendship, Courtship, Loveship, Marriage* (2001), has brought her a second Commonwealth Writers' Prize for her region (*Friend of My Youth* won in 1991). Harold Bloom includes *Something I've Been Meaning to Tell You* (1974) in his 'canonical prophecy' for Canadian literature.[1]

But Munro's entry into the international canon has been long delayed. Born in 1931, she is a contemporary of Toni Morrison and John Updike, both of whom are far more familiar to literature students and to the general reader. One reason for this is her Canadian nationality. Just as Canadians abroad are mistaken for Americans (see 'The Jack Randa Hotel', *Open Secrets*), so Canadian writing in English is sometimes subsumed into US or British literature. Another is the tendency to measure intellectual achievement according to bulk. Canada's best-known literary export, Margaret Atwood, receives more attention for her increasingly lengthy novels than for her innovative short fiction.

1

The misconception that short stories are apprentice pieces, aborted novels, still persists, exerting artistic pressures both from publishers and from within. Many Munro stories began with the attempt at a novel, and her second book, the linked sequence *Lives of Girls and Women* (1971), is still classified as such. Even now, she sets her sights on full-length fiction, only half joking when she says, 'My ambition is to write a novel before I die'.[2] Speaking three years before the appearance of *The Love of a Good Woman*, she describes her work in progress as a novel.[3]

If Munro kept to her plans, producing something that approached a conventional novel, the results might be more easily assimilated into the mainstream, but they would be far less interesting. Instead, she splices together seemingly disparate narratives within a single story. This can be seen in those longer stories which are almost novellas – 'The Love of a Good Woman', 'Carried Away' and the 'Chaddeleys and Flemings' sequence in *The Moons of Jupiter* (1982). But this deliberate fragmentation is at work in all her stories. What begins as a simple anecdote, a character sketch or a memoir, digresses into additional material, rival versions and other viewpoints. The truth is never fully told. One story generates another; and this sense of incompletion suggests a contingent, ongoing reality which ultimately escapes definition.

At 18, Munro aspired to write 'the Great Canadian Novel'.[4] Canadian authors share the postcolonial dilemma with writers from other parts of the former British Empire, from India to Africa, the Caribbean and Australasia – how to assert a distinctive identity, either rejecting or re-interpreting the colonial inheritance. For Canadians, this dilemma is compounded by their proximity to the world's dominant superpower, the US.

Canada's literary culture is distinguished by its diversity. Munro's own family background is Scots and Protestant Irish. Her stories are mostly set in Huron County, southwestern Ontario, where she was born, and where she returned as an adult. It is an area marked by a strong Scottish Presbyterian presence, as she records in stories like 'Friend of My Youth' (*Friend of My Youth*) and 'A Wilderness Station' (*Open Secrets*). But Munro's Scottish heritage goes beyond subject matter. As she discovered later in life, she is related to James Hogg (1770–1835), author of *Confessions of a Justified Sinner* and to Margaret Hogg, his mother, famous for her knowledge of ancient ballads and folk tales. The Hoggs represent an approach to storytelling which dwells on the fantastic, and the grotesque, and which is driven by a compelling oral voice. 'A Wilderness Station', 'Friend of My Youth' and less overtly Scottish stories like 'The Love of a Good Woman' (*The Love of a Good Woman*) incorporate chilling oral accounts of violence and misdeeds. Munro has sometimes been classified as a realist, documenting everyday experience. But she also has a penchant for the gothic, which may be linked to elements in Scottish culture.

Along with many teenagers, Munro was obsessed by *Wuthering Heights*, another gothic text which, like the *Confessions*, is suffused with Calvinist imagery. As a former literature student and an avid lifelong reader, Munro is very familiar with canonical writers such as Tennyson, Hardy, Lawrence and Joyce. The stories often respond to their work from a female perspective, sometimes as an act of homage, and sometimes treating them with scepticism. 'Carried Away' can be seen as a reworking of Hardy's 'An Imaginative Woman', while 'Jakarta' (*The Love of a Good Woman*) challenges Lawrence's views on the feminine role, as voiced in 'The Fox'.

For Munro, reading and writing are closely intertwined. As well as appropriating the established male canon, her work pays tribute to other women writers. Her liking for the grotesque draws her to American 'Southern Gothic' writers, such as Flannery O'Connor, Carson McCullers and Eudora Welty. She has spoken about an affinity between rural and small-town existence in the American South and in southwestern Ontario. The debt owed by the early Munro to Welty's stories in *The Golden Apples* has been widely noticed; the title story in *Dance of the Happy Shades* (1968) seems to have been partially inspired by Welty's 'June Recital'. There are also echoes of the Texan writer Katherine Anne Porter in a later story, 'Open Secrets' (*Open Secrets*). I discuss 'Open Secrets' at greater length in chapter 5. In the meantime, it is worth noting that the mood of suppressed violence in a hard-working and insular rural community recalls Porter's 'Noon Wine', in her

3

Pale Horse, Pale Rider collection (1939). Like Munro, Porter registers the force of public opinion, whether spoken, repressed or internalized. In 'Noon Wine', a farmer is acquitted of murder, yet, believing himself condemned by his neighbours, later commits suicide. 'Open Secrets' uses another supposed murder to explore themes of guilt and retribution, but it is less the details of plot than the hidden violence, and the connections drawn between public tittle-tattle and internal insights, that link the stories together. Summers are hot in Ontario; the stifling atmosphere in Munro's story would not be out of place in the Deep South. Another influence is Willa Cather, whose Canadian visits are mentioned in 'Dulse' (*The Moons of Jupiter*).

In *The Lonely Voice*, Frank O'Connor argues that the short story gives a voice to outsiders, and that it flourishes in underdeveloped areas or regions on the edge of powerful civilizations.[5] The American women writers admired by Munro engaged with frontier life as they charted the experiences of pioneers and their close descendants. Munro follows in this female tradition, using, as they often did, short fiction and story sequences to evoke places and characters to which we may return, in an open-ended structure like those used by oral storytellers.

The short story affirms local identities but it may also be seen as an international genre. In chapter 3, I examine Munro's relationship to the modernist writers whose techniques defined short-story form at the start of the twentieth century. Katherine Mansfield and James Joyce wrote about their native lands, but lived migratory lives in Europe. They were themselves following on from what Chekhov had achieved in Russia or Maupassant in France. As I observe in chapter 2, Munro's return to her hometown after some years in British Columbia coincided with her widening exposure in the US. Paradoxically, regular publication in the *New Yorker* guaranteed an outlet for work which, according to Munro, was regarded as limited and provincial by the Canadian literary élite.

Both in the short story and in the novel, Canadian fiction roams across national boundaries. Another distinguished contributor to the *New Yorker* is Mavis Gallant, whose stories are set mostly in Europe; she has lived in Paris for half a century.

Writers such as Michael Ondaatje, Rohinton Mistry and Anne Michaels explore their own origins, and also use fiction to bring together experiences across the globe. Ondaatje's novel *The English Patient* challenges the whole concept of rigid national affiliations. Migrating between different lands and cultures, Canadian writers often suggest that identity itself is in perpetual transition. In her introduction to *The Oxford Book of Canadian Short Stories in English* (1986), Margaret Atwood comments that, like other former colonies, Canada undergoes 'a collision between a landscape and social history not at first indigenous to it, with each side altering the other'.[6] Because the land itself is so 'vast, northern and cold', it is unimaginable, and this inaccessibility is also extended to concepts of home and of self.

Munro's work combines the international with the provincial. It also integrates a literary voice with oral testimony, another common characteristic in Canadian literature. The pioneers' need to record their own experience has given rise to a pronounced oral historical strand, evident, for instance, in Alistair Macleod. Nineteenth-century sketches of local life, animal tales and natural history initiated a short-story tradition based on observation and anecdote. Stephen Leacock's humorous tales, collected in *Sunshine Sketches of a Little Town* (1912) and other volumes, drew successfully on this provincial material.

When Munro's father, Robert Laidlaw, began writing, shortly before his death, he naturally produced memoirs and historical pieces, culminating in a novel, *The McGregors: A Novel of an Ontario Pioneer Family*. This was published posthumously in 1979. Laidlaw's aim was to reconstruct a vanished way of life, down to the details of farming practices, social rituals, food and drink. In *Lives of Girls and Women*, Munro sees the quest for authenticity as ultimately self-defeating: 'the hope of accuracy we bring to such tasks is crazy, heartbreaking' (*LGW* 249). The attempt to capture 'real life' (Munro's original title for her book) simply generates uncertainties about the truth. Like many other immigrants, Robert Laidlaw's forebears left behind letters and memoirs. 'A Wilderness Station' is loosely based on one of these first-hand accounts. But in Munro's hands competing versions of events proliferate. Far from authenticating experience, individual testimonies complicate the past.

Although she frequently cites L. M. Montgomery's *Emily of New Moon* as a formative influence, Munro appears to be less conscious of a broader Canadian identity than her pioneering inheritance. As an Ontarian, she sometimes speaks about the time she spends in British Columbia as a kind of exile. This is not altogether surprising, in such a large country; as she herself has pointed out, Montgomery's Prince Edward Island is a world away from Lake Huron. Nonetheless, her work can be placed within the context of national self-assertion, following World War II. Robert Weaver's CBC radio programme *Canadian Short Stories*, a major outlet for Munro's work during the fifties, marked the beginning of a flowering in Canadian literary culture. During the sixties and seventies, an expansion in Canadian publishing, broadcasting and in literary magazines, fostered by the countercultural mood of the time, promoted short fiction by writers such as Clark Blaise and Rudy Wiebe, and, especially, by women, including Marian Engel, Margaret Laurence Audrey Thomas and Margaret Atwood. The growth in women's writing was largely a consequence of 'second wave' feminism, and the upheavals in personal relationships brought about by the sexual revolution. Many of the newer writers were primarily interested in formal experimentation, another reason why Munro felt herself excluded from literary coteries as someone harking back to an outmoded regional tradition.

Literary criticism can sometimes be a search for unity, identifying key themes and revealing a basic trajectory informing a writer's whole oeuvre. To an extent, this is inevitable. But, given the nature of Munro's writing, I have avoided trying to slot her into neat categories. As I show in my opening chapters, Munro distrusts the artistic impulse to shape experience into closed forms which are aesthetically satisfying but place limits on reality. (She also perceives a human propensity to read our own lives, and those of others, as if they fitted such easy patterns.) Munro's stories defy simple definitions. Even though they are firmly rooted in the quotidian, they engage with the numinous and the intangible. Critics often cite a 1974 magazine article, in which she writes:

I am still partly convinced that this river – not even the whole river but this little stretch of it – will provide whatever myths you want, whatever adventures. I name the plants, I name the fish, and every name seems to me triumphant, every leaf and quick fish remarkably valuable. This ordinary place is sufficient, everything here touchable and mysterious.   (EH)

Munro's fascination with an elusive and complex reality has developed into an exploration of parallel worlds and multiple perspectives, especially in *Open Secrets* (1994). But while the mapping of alternative realities might suggest postmodern strategies, her strongly personal voice, with its distinctive lyricism, is at variance with the postmodern play of surfaces.

Munro has been very much a writer's writer, as the tributes on her covers testify. Joyce Carol Oates, A. S. Byatt, Richard Ford, Carol Shields and John Updike see her work as a touchstone for literary excellence. Ford included her twice in his 1990 anthology, *Best American Short Stories*. According to Cynthia Ozick, 'she is our Chekhov and is going to outlast most of her contemporaries'.[7] What so impresses Munro's peers is the lucidity of her style. Her carefully nuanced language combines literary sophistication with the vigour of everyday speech. There is nothing gimmicky about her work. By staying out of fashion, she has moved beyond it.

For Munro, storytelling is not a linear process. It is more like exploring a house than wandering down a straight road: 'Everybody knows what a house does, how it encloses space and makes connections between one enclosed space and another, and presents what is outside in a new way' (WR). In keeping with that spirit, I make connections across her work, rather than attempting a strictly chronological survey.

There is another reason to be selective. Because short fiction – especially Munro's fiction – is so densely written, every page is crowded with potential interpretations. Any attempt to be comprehensive, on my part, would be futile. Instead, I prefer to give detailed readings of individual stories, which may offer comparative insights into work I have not analysed. Chapter 1 combines a reading of Munro's second book, *Lives of Girls and Women*, with a look at a more recent story, from *The Love of a Good Woman*. Both are concerned with the making of a female artist. Munro's own biographical background is addressed in the second chapter, which uses *Who Do You Think You Are?* – rechristened *The Beggar Maid* in the US and Great Britain – to relate Munro's aesthetic practice to an ambivalence towards artistic self-expression, which is related to class and gender. This chapter also examines 'The Peace of Utrecht' (*Dance of the Happy Shades*, 1968), as a key text in Munro's exploration of the mother–daughter dyad. The emphasis elsewhere is primarily, though not exclusively, on more recent stories from *Open Secrets* and *The Love of a Good Woman*.

The main theme of this book is Munro's treatment of time and memory. Chapter 3 explores the ability of the short story, as a genre, to engage with the passing moment. It shows how Munro both utilizes and subverts modernist techniques, such as the epiphany, which exploited that ability. I have found Bakhtinian concepts about dialogue, carnival and double-voice discourse a helpful way of describing the many competing voices at work in each of the stories. I introduce these ideas in chapter 4, which also explains how silence can be as eloquent as speech. Chapter 5 looks at narrative structure, asking whether there are turning points and patterns of cause and effect in the stories, while chapter 6 discusses how memory creates conflicting versions of the past. In the final chapter, I show how Munro's latest collection, *Hateship, Friendship, Courtship, Loveship, Marriage* (2001), faces up to the ageing process, placing this book in relation to her abiding fascination with the grotesque and what Kristeva calls the abject. Time brings decay, but it also brings renewal, and Munro's work continues to embrace the unpredictable, whatever surprises the future has in store.

1

Looking at the Moon:
The Female Artist

Lives of Girls and Women (1971) is Munro's *Portrait of the Artist*. At an early stage in her own career, she traces the emergence of a writer's sensibility and declares her artistic manifesto. The adolescent Del reads in a magazine that the psychological differences between men and women may be illustrated by the image of a boy and girl on a park bench looking at the full moon: 'The boy thinks of the universe, its immensity and mystery; the girl thinks "I must wash my hair" ' (*LGW* 177). Del is frantic:

> I wanted men to love me, *and* I wanted to think of the universe when I looked at the moon. I felt trapped, stranded; it seemed there had to be a choice where there couldn't be a choice . . . *For a woman, everything is personal; no idea is of any interest to her by itself, but must be translated into her own experience; in works of art she always sees her own life, or her daydreams.* (*LGW* 178)

Del's mother Addie shrugs off such 'male nonsense' (*LGW* 17), denying any intrinsic difference between the sexes. Addie earns her living selling encyclopaedias. She advocates what Julia Kristeva has described as first-stage feminism[1] which, in calling for equality through social legislation, ultimately internalizes male values. She writes embarrassing letters to the local paper, promoting women's rights and opposing compulsory religious education.

Addie's rationalism is at odds with Del's romantic ideals. She quizzes her mother about her marriage to her father, repeating the phrase 'in love' – 'But you fell in love with him',

'You fell in love', 'Why did you fall in love?' (*LGW* 78). Addie remains evasive, speaking more in terms of etiquette than the emotions: 'Your father was always a gentleman'. She often seems more at home in the social than the personal. Her commitment to a public identity, in her role as letter-writer, contrasts with Del's immersion in private passions. Del will not give up the discourse of 'love'. The word is repeated obsessively, as her erotic self-absorption diverts her from the academic success that Addie wants for her daughter:

> *She is in love. She has just come from being with her lover. She has given herself to her lover. Seed runs down her legs.* (*LGW* 228)

Like Sylvia Plath's heroine Esther Greenwood, in her novel *The Bell Jar* (1963), Del hungers for sexual experience. Del's transformation into a fantasy self as she loses her virginity resembles Esther's conviction that a 'spectacular change' will come over her when she crosses the 'boundary line'.[2] Both heroines, and both writers, assert their femininity, while struggling against the restrictive definitions of sexual difference imposed by conventional wisdom. Esther also reacts strongly to a magazine article, this time cut out by her mother from the *Reader's Digest*: 'a man's world is different from a woman's world and a man's emotions are different from a woman's emotions and only marriage can bring the two worlds and the two different sets of emotions together properly'.[3] Although Del refuses to seek fulfilment in the type of cerebral, androgynous identity Addie's feminism seems to offer, it would be wrong to see mother and daughter as polar opposites. The names form two halves of a whole ('Adele'). As well as the socially responsible missives she sends to the local press, Addie also publishes letters in the women's page of a city newspaper, 'full of long decorative descriptions of the countryside from which she had fled' (*LGW* 80). Despite her internalization of male values, she resorts here to a stereotypically feminine style: '*This morning a marvelous silver frost enraptures the eye on every twig and telephone wire and makes the world a veritable fairyland*' (*LGW* 80).

There are further contradictions. Addie signs these letters 'Princess Ida', a name borrowed from Tennyson's bluestocking heroine, thus signalling her first-stage feminism. Yet the name also echoes the title of Gilbert and Sullivan's lampoon; and it is worth remembering that Tennyson's *The Princess* ends with Ida giving up her studies when she falls in love.

At the end of her affair, Del speaks a line from *Mariana* into the mirror: 'He cometh not, she said' (*LGW* 238). The quotation comes from Addie's *Complete Tennyson*, passed on, in matrilineal succession, from her former teacher. Del says the line 'with absolute sincerity, absolute irony', the oxymoron balancing faith with detachment. She is both rejecting and accepting the masochistic solipsism she reads in *Mariana*, whose heroine waits endlessly for the man who abandoned her. Superficially, Del picks herself up and acts sensibly, circling jobs adverts in a methodical manner. But even as she discards fantasy, it re-emerges: 'Now at last without fantasy or self-deception, cut off from the mistakes and confusion of the past, grave and simple, carrying a small suitcase, like girls in movies leaving home, convents, lovers, I supposed I would get started on my real life' (*LGW* 238).

Del's mirror also suggests another Tennyson heroine, the Lady of Shalott who, like Mariana, is suspended in isolation as she waits for her life to be activated. And while Addie's 'Princess Ida' persona displays a stereotypically feminine sensitivity to nature, it is also another aspect of her need for public recognition – albeit pseudonymously. Already, in the story 'Princess Ida', Del recognizes that 'I myself was not so different from my mother, but concealed it, knowing what dangers there were' (*LGW* 80). The danger, for both women, lies in standing out from the crowd, in displaying the strength of their desires.

'Real life' means external reality, the everyday routines accessed by Del's pencil marks around the advertisements for telephone operators out there in the city. But it is also the *Real Life* which, at the end of the 'Baptizing' story is italicized alongside the name of Del's lover, *Garnet French* (*LGW* 238). This *Real Life* runs beyond the quotidian.

In her pioneering study, *The Second Sex* (1949), the French feminist Simone de Beauvoir castigates the typical woman writer for yielding to an ultimately self-limiting narcissism: 'It is her own self', she says, 'that is the principal – sometimes the unique subject of interest to her'.[4] This is not unlike the female

11

mentality pictured in Del's magazine. Del's response – 'I wanted men to love me, *and* I wanted to think of the universe' (*LGW* 178) – refuses to make the stark choice between emotional and intellectual fulfilment.

In the final story, 'Epilogue: The Photographer', Del transposes the lives of her neighbours into a gothic yarn. In this uncompleted novel, Del is both subject and object – both the photographer himself and his image, Caroline, based on Marion Sherriff, a local suicide. Caroline, like Bizet's Carmen in 'Baptizing', is a projection of Del's own sexuality, treating men with 'tender contempt, indifferent readiness' (*LGW* 243). The photographer is the male artist, the sinister outsider who has no name, and who mysteriously disappears, leaving the pregnant Caroline to destroy herself. Male and female are irreconcilable within the dynamic that Del has constructed.

Del's novel seems 'true to me, not real but true, as if I had discovered, not made up, such people and such a story, as if that town was lying close behind the one I walked through every day' (*LGW* 244). But when she is invited onto the Sherriffs' porch by Marion's brother, Bobby, the fiction-making process begins to seem inadequate. In the commonplace details of the Sherriffs' house, Del recognizes a reality as complex and ineluctable as fantasy. Talking to Bobby about her own plans, she starts to wonder what happened, not to her invention, Caroline, but to the living Marion; and what will happen to Bobby, a polite, ineffectual young man, recently released from the asylum. 'Such questions persist, in spite of novels' (*LGW* 247).

The ceaseless flow of experience resists definition. The artist's attempt to transcend time, capturing 'every last thing, every layer of speech and thought, stroke of light on bark or walls, every small pothole, pain, crack, delusion, held still and held together – radiant, everlasting' (*LGW* 249) is doomed to frustration. Life is protean and contradictory – 'dull, simple, amazing and unfathomable – deep caves paved with kitchen linoleum'. Wishing her luck as Bobby takes her plate away, he rises on his toes 'like a plump ballerina':

This action, accompanied by his delicate smile, appeared to be a joke not shared with me so much as displayed for me, and it seemed also to have a concise meaning – a stylized meaning – to be a letter, or a whole word, in an alphabet I did not know.   (*LGW* 249–50)

The secret 'concise meaning' is part of a whole network of multiple signs, which can never be fully decoded. Del is learning empathy; her neighbours are not inert material, waiting to be processed by the artistic imagination. Neither can their lives be simply recorded factually, through the lists of streets and names that Del will attempt later on, when she has left her hometown. It is in the dialogue between solid reality ('kitchen linoleum') and the unknowable consciousness of others ('deep caves') that Munro's fiction is generated. Del's growing fascination with the unverifiable – Marion's 'act and her secrecy', 'the few poor facts and everything that was not told' (*LGW* 246, 247), Bobby's concealed joke – signals an exploration of secrecy and silence at the heart of Munro's work.

The figure of the female artist recurs in stories like 'Material' (*Something I've Been Meaning to Tell You*, 1974) and 'Meneseteung' (*Friend of My Youth*, 1990), and as Rose, the actress, in *The Beggar Maid* (1978). A recent incarnation is as Jill, the musician, in 'My Mother's Dream' (*The Love of a Good Woman*, 1998). Jill is a violinist, and she is also the story's eponymous mother. Like so many of Munro's stories, it shifts in time and space, beginning with what at first appears to be an awakening:

During the night – or during the time she had been asleep – there had been a heavy fall of snow.
   My mother looked out from a big arched window such as you find in a mansion or an old fashioned public building. She looked down on lawns and shrubs, hedges, flower gardens, trees, all covered by snow that lay in heaps and cushions, not levelled or disturbed by wind. The white of it did not hurt your eyes as it does in sunlight. The white was the white of snow under a clear sky just before dawn.   (*TLGW* 293)

As the sense of calm turns into disorientation, it soon becomes apparent that Jill is dreaming. The season is out of kilter, with green leaves visible under the snow; she is in a strange place, abandoned by people she can't quite remember. All she knows for sure is that somewhere in this alien landscape she has left a baby. As she searches for her child, she crosses imperceptibly into her waking life:

> The snow and the leafy gardens and the strange house had all withdrawn. The only remnant of the whiteness was the blanket in the crib. A baby blanket of light white wool, crumpled halfway down the baby's back. In the heat, the real summer heat, the baby was wearing only a diaper and a pair of plastic pants to keep the sheet dry. The plastic pants had a pattern of butterflies.
>
> My mother, still thinking no doubt about the snow and the cold that usually accompanies snow, pulled the blanket up to cover the baby's bare back and shoulders, its red-downed head. (*TLGW* 295)

The tense then changes from past to present, and the indeterminacy of the dream gives way to the specific space–time co-ordinates of 'the real world. The world of July 1945' (*TLGW* 295). We are in a 'one-and-a-half-story' white wooden house, cramped, but respectable' in 'a small town that is indistinguishable . . . from a lot of other small towns to be found ten or fifteen miles apart in the once thickly populated farmland near Lake Huron' (*TLGW* 296). This is where the narrator's father grew up, and where Jill has joined his family – 'and I joined them too, being large and lively inside her – after my father was killed in the final weeks of the war in Europe' (*TLGW* 296).

The narrative then shifts back in time, to the day of the funeral, and goes on to detail Jill's struggle to cope both with her new family and the demands of a young baby. The temporal and spatial fluidity introduced by the dream passage recurs throughout the story. But what is most striking about 'My Mother's Dream' is the split in identities signalled by the variations in names and pronouns – 'a baby', 'her baby', 'me', 'my mother', 'Jill'. The narrator is Jill's child, looking back to a time just before her own birth and just afterwards. She may be physically present, in the womb or the cradle, but any consciousness she may experience, in that pre-linguistic state, is withheld from the reader. The narrative is focalized mostly through the mother, Jill. The narrator has no name.

At the funeral, the pregnant Jill is desperately hungry. Her subjective experience is rendered exactly, through sensuous descriptions of hamburgers and custard tarts. The use of the present tense adds immediacy, as physical reactions turn into complex interior states: 'When her real hunger is satisfied her imaginary hunger is still working, and even more an irritability amounting almost to panic that makes her stuff into her mouth what she can hardly taste any longer' (*TLGW* 297).

The re-introduction of the past tense accompanies a movement from an internal to a more external, historical form of discourse: 'She had known for some time about me and she also knew that George Kirkham might be killed'. The narrative continues to shift between tenses and viewpoints, briefly refocalized through a neighbour, Mrs Shantz, and later through an aunt, Ailsa; but mostly switching between mother and daughter. It is never clear how much of this might be Jill's memories, passed on to her daughter, and what might be speculation, as the narrator filters her mother's past through her imagination. As in *Lives of Girls and Women*, identities cross within the mother–daughter dyad, even though they are superficially opposed.

Jill is an orphan. The self-sufficiency that she has learnt from living without family ties expresses itself through her musicianship. At school, her concentration on the violin is regarded as a substitute for a social life; she is encouraged to be 'normal' and 'well rounded' (*TLGW* 310). Her in-laws are also threatened by her autonomy, and distrustful towards classical music. But her real trials begin when the baby is born. As if siding with convention, she screams when Jill tries to practise. She has already refused Jill's milk, preferring to take the bottle from her neurasthenic aunt, Iona. The violin raises her aversion to Jill into outright hostility.

When the in-laws go away on an overnight trip, the baby is impossible to soothe. In desperation, Jill returns to the violin: 'stuck in a prison of my making, she thinks of a space of her own, an escape within' (*TLGW* 323). But her playing is dreadful: 'the violin is bewitched, it hates her' (*TLGW* 324). She is rejected both by her child and her instrument; the distorted music echoes the baby's howl. Jill's anger is boundless, both on this occasion and after her first attempt to pick up the violin: 'in a fairy tale she would have risen off the bed with the strength of a young giantess and gone through the house breaking furniture and necks' (*TLGW* 319); she shoves violin and bow under the sofa 'because she has a picture of herself smashing and wrecking them against a chair back, in a sickening dramatic display' (*TLGW* 324). Both the adult and the infant are possessed by a primitive rage, driven by their own self-centred instincts.

In despair, Jill gives both herself and her child some sleeping pills. It is in the sleep that follows that she has the dream. The next morning, she wakes up to Iona's screaming; finding the child preternaturally still, she believes that Jill has smothered her. For a few pages, the reader shares the misconception. (A dead narrator is unusual, but not impossible). However, Jill discovers her alive, left under the sofa, next to the violin; Iona put her there when a terrified Ailsa refused to look at the supposed corpse.

The incident marks the real beginning of the maternal bond, and an ending to the opposition between motherhood and creativity. The violin is safely stowed away, and the child waits peacefully to be fed. It is also a turning point in the narrator's life:

> To me it seems that it was only then that I became female . . . I believe that it was only at the moment when I decided to come back, when I gave up the fight against my mother (which must have been a fight for something like her total surrender) and when in fact I chose survival over victory (death would have been victory), that I took on my female nature.
> And to some extent Jill took on hers. (*TLGW* 337)

The interval between Iona's screaming (*TLGW* 327) and the discovery of the child alive under the sofa (*TLGW* 333) is not simply a means of creating suspense in the reader. The storyteller's ability to resolve events is also a configuration of the infant's unconscious power over life and death. 'Survival over victory' is a resonant phrase, in a wartime context, reversing the conventional male priorities.

Towards the end of the story, the snowy imagery from the dream is reprised in 'the white mass of dough' at the bakery where the narrator, as a child, watches Iona working; and in Iona's white apron, the great white kitchen and the icing on wedding cakes (*TLGW* 338). The whiteness 'shifted and bubbled like something alive'. Snow, like the white blanket over the sleeping baby, conceals the life seething beneath. White, the colour of snow, frost and moonlight, suggests mystery, magic and transformation. In 'White Dump' (*The Progress of Love*), children scramble over a glistening, almost heavenly white mountain of icing and marshmallow from the biscuit factory. Whiteness is especially appropriate to the dream states evoked so often in Munro's stories. Her dreamers attain a detachment, remote from their waking lives. The dream landscape may be baffling, but it is supremely calm and peaceful. In an introduction to her 1996 *Selected Stories*, she describes watching a farmer unload grain from a horse-drawn sleigh, when she was about 15.[5] The vibrant picture of falling snow, grain and mud seems to have struck her forcefully, as a glimpse of life on the move, something almost impossible to capture. Snow is, of course, a very Canadian image.

There are indications in 'My Mother's Dream' that there is nothing so very much amiss, and that the whole crisis is produced by repressive attitudes in that 'cramped but respectable' household. Iona leaps into action as soon as the baby makes its first, fairly faint, cries; the entire family panics when she reacts to Jill's playing. These are the same conformist attitudes that dismiss classical music itself; and which Addie flouts, in *Lives of Girls and Women*, when she puts herself on public display.

Both mother and baby yield to passions which Iona, Ailsa and their senile mother subdue in themselves and fear in others. The adult narrator suggests that there was nothing pathological in her early behaviour, and that Jill's own anxiety blots out common sense when she's left alone; she never registers that the squalling baby might be simply suffering from the heat. 'What is it about an infant's crying', she wonders, 'that makes it so powerful, so able to break down the order you depend on, inside and outside yourself?' (*TLGW* 322). Jill's artistic passion is also cool and measured. Music is 'a problem ... that she has to work out strictly and daringly, and that she has taken on as her responsibility in life' (*TLGW* 319–20). When her child survives, she accepts a second responsibility 'because the alternative to loving was disaster' (*TLGW* 337). In years to come, she will continue to play professionally, despite a second marriage and subsequent pregnancies.

Munro's fiction presents time as a continuum, in which past and present merge, and identities intermingle. Our consciousness of ourselves is generated largely through our relationship with others. In *Lives of Girls and Women* and 'My Mother's Dream', the mother–daughter dyad exemplifies this shifting subjectivity. In *Lives of Girls and Women*, re-imagining other lives emerges as the writer's task, undertaken in the knowledge that 'real life' will always escape definition. Such a model of creativity is a long way from de Beauvoir's portrait of the narcissistic woman writer; yet it does not require the female artist to renounce passion. Libidinal drives interact with a sense of order and detachment, as Jill finds when she plays the violin. Both our own experiences and those of others are multiplicitous; we can contemplate the universe and still remember to wash our hair.

2

The Biographical Background

Alice Munro called her fourth book *Who Do You Think You Are?*
In the title story, her protagonist, Rose, hasn't bothered
copying out a poem because she has already learnt it by heart.
Here, as so often in her work, Munro unlocks a turn of phrase
to examine what lies behind it. Rose has a semi-rural upbring-
ing similar to Munro's own background in southwestern
Ontario. This is a world where you do not call attention to
yourself; you keep your head down, and get on with the job.
It is a culture on the margins, where those who slip between
social classes guard their status nervously; and steel themselves for disappointment by not hoping for too much.

In an early interview with Graeme Gibson, Munro speaks
about being raised in a community 'two or three generations
away from being pioneers',[1] where practical skills are more
valuable than introspection. Self-revelation invites ridicule;
following the Calvinist tradition of their Scottish forebears,
local people regard artistic beauty as a dangerous distraction.
Rose becomes an actress – a professional show-off. Alice
Laidlaw became Alice Munro, the writer, adopting her first
husband's name.

Alice Laidlaw was born in 1931. Although her mother, Anne,
had worked as a schoolteacher, and – spurred by his daughter's success – her father later produced a family saga, this was
not a bookish environment. Robert Laidlaw raised foxes and
mink for their fur, which his wife sometimes sold around local
resorts. In the Gibson interview, Munro claims that most of her
relatives still dismiss artistic expression as pointless self-
indulgence. She describes writing as an escape and a disguise,
evolved during childhood. But despite this sense of alienation,

she has always shown great empathy for the people she grew up with, and, since the mid-seventies, has lived mostly within the area where she was born. This is partly because of the landscape, something she often refers to in interviews. The farmlands of southwestern Ontario are not, by her account, exceptionally beautiful. They do not compare with the more spectacular, mountainous geography of British Columbia. But she gains a sense of freedom from its expansiveness, and she has also spoken about the benefits of intimacy with a particular place and its people.

There is something else which may, perhaps, keep her close to home – a sense in which the attitudes she inherited have been absorbed into her work. The preoccupation with material reality, and with utility, becomes a fascination with commonplace objects – such as the optometrist's instruments at the start of 'The Love of a Good Woman'. Her stories plumb beneath the surface, but they also suggest that sufficiency in the external world evoked by her article 'Everything Here is Touchable and Mysterious'. In *Let Us Now Praise Famous Men*, the American writer James Agee tries to find a verbal equivalent for the documentary photographs published alongside his account of rural deprivation. ' "Description" ', he says, 'is a word to suspect. Words cannot embody. They can only describe'.[2] His prose bears witness, like the photographs, to a face or a homestead or a pair of boots, letting the unadorned image speak for itself. Language, too, becomes an object of curiosity, like the 'found' objects used in art installations. Munro's characters often stop to handle an idiom – 'mood elevator', 'coup de grace', 'the chop' ('Lichen', *PL* 43); 'bizarre', 'bazaar', 'flipped his wig' ('Pictures of the Ice', in *Friend of My Youth*) – turning over a word again, and again, like something spotted in a junk shop.

American editors changed the *Who Do You Think You Are?* into *The Beggar Maid*, believing that the phrase would have little resonance outside Canada. It was under the second title that the collection was shortlisted for the Booker Prize in the UK. This short-story sequence, tracing a life from childhood to middle age, marks a symbolic turning point in Munro's career, highlighting the generic and personal ambivalence that has shaped both the writing and its reception.

According to Paul de Man, autobiography is 'a figure of reading or understanding that occurs, to some degree, in all texts'.[3] Because Munro's fiction incorporates confessional and biographical forms of discourse, and uses material which is clearly identifiable with her own background, it is tempting to match the stories to the 'real' Alice Munro. Despite the post-structural 'death of the author', de Man's 'figure of understanding' dominates the popular response to fiction more than ever. Academic criticism has discarded the notion that a text is the unmediated product of a uniquely constituted subject. Yet market demands have turned every author into a minor celebrity, promoting their books through interviews, profiles and personal appearances. Writers are obliged to make available a unified public persona, consistent with perceptions of their work. Moreover, Munro first began to be widely published during the seventies, at a time when 'second wave' feminism placed special value on the notion of uncovering lives that had been suppressed or distorted by a patriarchal tradition. Personal testimony was seen as politically empowering for both readers and writers.

Following on from this legacy, some critics, for instance Beverley Rasporich and Catherine Sheldrick Ross,[4] have greeted Munro's writing as the direct voice of female experience. A number of personal themes and images are re-investigated throughout her work, and their familiarity supports biographical readings. The clearest example is the mother–daughter nexus, which Magdalene Redekop sees as the source of Munro's aesthetic.[5]

Munro's mother provides what she herself has called 'my central material in life' (PR), the personal material which, she believes, activates her most powerful fiction. Written shortly after Anne Laidlaw's death from Parkinson's disease, in 1959, 'The Peace of Utrecht' has been identified – not least by its author – as a watershed in her development as a writer. 'The Peace of Utrecht' is the penultimate story in Munro's first collection, Dance of the Happy Shades (1968). A first-person narrative, written mostly in the present tense, it resembles a letter or a diary. As Helen recalls her dead mother's illness and imagines her sister Maddy's feelings about staying at home to nurse her, while she herself has moved away and married, she

21

deconstructs the whole process of memory. Maddy and Helen conceal their differences in a mutual fantasy – 'that version of our childhood which is safely preserved in anecdote, as in a kind of mental cellophane' (DHS 193).

They talk continually, but they avoid discussing their mother, even though, throughout her long disability, they have formed a partnership, reversing the power relationship between the generations. Their mother has been managed like a child, robbed of her adult autonomy by muscular and vocal paralysis. The sisters feel publicly embarrassed by the symptoms of Parkinson's disease: 'Our Gothic Mother, with the cold appalling mask of the Shaking Palsy laid across her features, shuffling, weeping, devouring attention wherever she can get it, eyes dead and burning, fixed inward on herself' (DHS 200). Even when she is kept safely behind doors, the distorted sound of her voice is too much for the sisters to handle – 'the cry for help – undisguised, oh, shamefully undisguised and raw' (DHS 198).

The sisters repress their own emotions and subdue their mother's terror, nursing her efficiently but, as Helen remembers, without affection. Shame, in this story, as in so many subsequent stories by Munro, is double-edged. Shame at her mother's condition has rebounded on Helen, and is compounded by her guilt towards Maddy.

Seen from the vantage point of the 'ordinary world' – the world Helen inhabits with her family in Toronto – 'our Gothic Mother' seems like a fantasy, 'too terrible, unreal' to be true (DHS 201). She also knows that her mother's deterioration was not uniform, her symptoms not always so extreme. As she tries to piece together her contradictory memories, the narrative switches from the observational present-tense mode, in which she describes 'our Gothic Mother', to the past. Between observation and memoir, past and present, it enters into the timeless zone of the dream. On her better days, 'she has wakened out of a bad dream; she tries to make up for lost time, tidying the house, forcing her stiff trembling hands to work a little while at the sewing machine' (DHS 200). Since her death, it has been Helen's turn to dream of her mother performing these household tasks, 'and I think, why did I exaggerate so to myself, see, she is all right, only that her hands are trembling' (DHS 200).

Drawing on psychoanalytic theory and clinical observation, Nancy Choderow has concluded that the close identification between mother and daughter confuses ego boundaries, making it relatively difficult for women to construct an autonomous self.[6] Munro's work explores these overlapping subjectivities. The daughter's identity is inextricably bound to the maternal; Helen doubles for her mother in the dream. Yet the mother's inner self remains mysterious, and her image evades representation. In trying to come to terms with the contradictory and indistinct figure of the mother, her art is set in motion – not the static fiction-making which wraps experience in 'mental cellophane', but a dynamic engagement with an ever-changing reality.

Though fraught with personal danger, the mother–daughter dialogue is artistically productive. Bakhtin argues that all subjectivity is founded on dialogue with a putative other. 'I am not alone when I look at myself in the mirror: I am possessed by some one else's soul.'[7] Thus we 'author' our own selves. The ambivalent relationship between mother and daughter, between intimacy and estrangement, is deeply implicated in the evolution of self-awareness. It is also connected to concepts of 'shame', a word used frequently in Munro's fiction. In *The Beggar Maid*, Rose's bare-breasted appearance in a TV production of *The Trojan Women* ('Spelling') is simply one variety of the shame that she has courted since her education first took her away from home. Uncharacteristically taking pen to paper, her stepmother Flo writes to her. She tells her '*Shame*' (*BM* 190, emphasis Munro's).

Flo is not Anne Laidlaw. She and Rose's carping brother, Brian, speak generically for the communal forces of 'low-voiced contempt' (*BM* 183). But, once again, shame cuts both ways, as Rose discovers when she takes her boyfriend home:

> She felt ashamed on more levels than she could count. She was ashamed of the food and the swan and the plastic tablecloth; ashamed for Patrick, the gloomy snob, who made a startled grimace when Flo passed him the toothpick-holder; ashamed for Flo with her timidity and hypocrisy and pretensions; most of all ashamed for herself. (*BM* 90)

In the 'Princess Ida' section of *Lives of Girls and Women*, the adolescent Del cringes at the way her mother, an encyclopaedia saleswoman, proselytizes on progressive issues: 'Who else had a mother like that?' (*LGW* 79). Addie Jordan is blind to 'how contemptuous, how superior and silent and enviable they were, those people who all their lives could stay still, with no need to do or say anything remarkable' (*LGW* 80). Del yearns for the security of the herd, even though she sees through the herd mentality.

While Addie Jordan does not simply translate to Anne Laidlaw, both the referential and the fictional mother stand apart from their local communities. Speaking about her childhood on the outskirts of town, on the peripheries of the social structure, 'in a kind of little ghetto where all the bootleggers and prostitutes and hangers-on lived' (Tausky, p. ix). Munro puts the whole family in a 'community of outcasts'. Interviewed by the *Paris Review*, she describes the agonies of watching her mother trying to fit in with the ladies at the luncheon club. But marginalization, as we have seen, does not necessarily entail a wholesale rejection of the values by which you are judged. The smug majority are still 'enviable', and in Del, Rose and Helen, the rebel coexists with the conformist.

Shame is a dialogic process. Munro's heroines are alternately mortified by their mothers' behaviour and ashamed of their own response. It is a 'social emotion', implying public exposure.[8] But it is also voiced internally, and manifested physiologically, for instance through blushing. It is something learnt during infancy, usually through the mother.

In 'The Peace of Utrecht', shame is linked with the public display of private emotion. In 'Spelling', it suggests ambivalence about class allegiance and the creative process. Rose is ashamed of the way she tells anecdotes about her childhood to divert her middle-class cronies. This storytelling is clearly related to the ethics of writing fiction. In transforming her own culture into art, Rose betrays her own people in two ways. In the first place, she is breaking the taboo against public self-exposure. Secondly, she is, as Rose sees it, perpetrating a fraud, by simplifying, or even distorting reality.

In interviews, Munro sometimes applies concepts of fraudulence to her own trade. She has said that her first publishing successes blocked her writing, making her anxious that she couldn't live up to a spurious reputation. Munro makes relatively few public appearances. She suggests that this is partly from fear of becoming 'a gigantic fraud'.[9] Because a writer's personality is sublimated in their work, a striking public persona must be an imposture, compensating for a 'disappointing ordinariness'. Publication, in itself, may be a shameful act. In 'Family Furnishings' (*Hateship, Friendship, Courtship, Loveship, Marriage*, 2001), Munro describes the detachment with which a writer files away experience for future use, and the family's reaction to their lives being turned into fiction.

Anne Laidlaw did not read her daughter's work. Munro believes that, if her mother's illness and death had not intervened, she could not have published such personal material without causing a split in the family. So, while the stories are generated by the scarcely imaginable figure of the maternal, the biographical mother is necessarily excluded from reading them. Other stories which use the mother–daughter dyad to explore female subjectivity and the fiction-making process include 'The Progress of Love' (see chapter 6); 'Winter Wind', 'Memorial' and 'The Ottawa Valley' in *Something I've Been Meaning to Tell You* (1974); and the title story of *Friend of My Youth* (1990), which is dedicated to 'the memory of my mother'. In 'Friend of My Youth', Munro uses another recurrent dream to transcend time, reanimating the dead mother, and removing a 'woeful, impersonal mask' superimposed by illness. The workings of time and of memory complicate the exchange of identities still further. In this dream, the middle-aged narrator is the same age as in her waking life, although, like Munro, she lost her mother when she was in her twenties. She is catching up with the dead mother. But there is another mother, the young woman who existed before she was born, who is known only through the stories she tells about her past. These dreams, in Munro's fiction, are puzzling yet strangely reassuring, inducing calm and clarity in the dreamer, who is an observer rather than a participant. 'My Mother's Dream', which I discussed in the previous chapter, makes the mother the dreamer. As Munro herself ages, other stories, such as 'The Moons of Jupiter' (*The Moons of Jupiter*, 1982) and 'Save the Reaper' (*The Love of a Good Woman*, 1998), have looked at the daughter from the mother's perspective. It is now the daughter who is both another self and someone alien.

The characters and events in Munro's fiction do not correspond neatly with biographical facts. They have been shaped by other texts, as well as by lived experience. The schoolteacher Miss Farris in *Lives of Girls and Women* shares many characteristics with Miss Gowrie in Mary McCarthy's *Memories of a Catholic Girlhood*, an autobiography which prefigures many of the themes and motifs in Munro's book. However, the conditions in which her work has been produced are relevant to the ambivalence it expresses about artistic representation; and to questions of gender, class and genre.

Munro spent two years on a scholarship at the University of Western Ontario, leaving without a degree when the money ran out. By 20 she was married; by 21, she had her first baby. She was transforming herself into a suburban housewife in Vancouver. A recent story, 'Jakarta', describes a similar situation:

> It seemed to her that life went on, after you finished school, as a series of further examinations to be passed. The first one was getting married. If you hadn't done that by the time you were twenty-five, that examination had to all intents and purposes been failed. (*TLGW* 82)

Munro's strong sense of artistic vocation often seems to have been in conflict with a longing for conventional domesticity. These are 'the twin choices of my life, which were marriage and motherhood, or the black life of the artist' (Tausky, p. x). In her teenage years, while her mother was ill, Munro was doing the housework. The pressure to conform to a female stereotype and the practical demands of motherhood have both taken their toll; Munro has spoken about an especially bleak time in her mid to late twenties, when she was getting her first stories published, whilst also looking after two small children. A memoir from her daughter Sheila[10] gives a candid account of these conflicts. It describes her annoyance at having an application for babysitting money, to buy her time to write, turned down by the Canada Council. A travel grant might have been regarded more favourably; travelling is what writers are supposed to do.

In his essay 'Fires', Raymond Carver recalls an afternoon in the mid-sixties, spent trying to get his family's washing through the Laundromat, waiting in vain for a dryer to be free:

I remember thinking at that moment, amid the feelings of helpless frustration that had me close to tears, that nothing – and, brother, I mean nothing – that ever happened to me on this earth could come anywhere close, could possibly be as important to me, could make as much difference, as the fact that I had two children. And that I would always have them and always find myself in this position of unrelieved responsibility and permanent distraction.[11]

Carver realizes that his lifestyle is nothing like the lives of writers he admires; and that he is going to have to reconcile himself to domestic chaos, ridding himself of the illusion that, one day, things will change. The image of the writer, forged out of romanticism and reiterated by the beat movement, is that of a free spirit, living a bohemian life on the road; solitary and prone to self-destruction ('the black life of the artist'), but ultimately transcending earthly limitations. It is a potent male myth, challenged by Munro in her story 'Material'.

Yet childcare and home life offer more than sheer drudgery. A domestic space is multi-purpose. *Lives of Girls and Women* was written, by necessity, in the laundry room, because it was the warmest place. But since then Munro has chosen to work in the bedroom, kitchen, dining room or hallway, in preference to an area dedicated to writing. In a 1984 interview with Harold Horwood,[12] she expresses horror at the idea, fearing that it would put her under pressure to produce something tangible every time she sat at the desk. Perhaps a state of 'permanent distraction' is not incompatible with writing. Perhaps it releases another kind of creativity, and a different type of fiction, which is not segregated from the family wash. The *Paris Review* interview talks about 'working in my head' when she had no time to sit down and write. In her fiction, reading, writing and daydreaming are interconnected. The short story form obviously lends itself to short, intensive bursts of writing. I would also suggest that those snatched moments might be conducive towards an intuitive, less controlled way of writing, receptive to the sudden turns and random digressions we find in Munro. Her metaphor for the narrative process – 'everybody knows what a house does' (WR) – is grounded in the practicalities of her writing life. Flexibility in her writing time may have contributed towards the temporal fluidity in her stories.

Munro's first marriage lasted over twenty years; during the sixties, she and her husband Jim ran a bookshop in British Columbia. By the early seventies, her work was featured regularly in Canadian literary magazines, and on the radio. She had published two prize-winning books. But then the marriage broke up and she returned to Ontario, where she subsequently married a geographer, Gerald Fremlin; they currently keep two homes – in British Columbia and in Clinton, less than thirty miles from Munro's home town. The house in Clinton is the place where Fremlin was born.

Munro's breakthrough as a writer for an international audience coincided with this return to her roots. After her third collection, *Something I've Been Meaning to Tell You* (1974), she was approached by an American agent, Virginia Barber, who started placing stories in the *New Yorker* and raised her profile with American publishers. Despite winning the Governor General's Award, *Dance of the Happy Shades* did not outsell its Canadian print run – a mere two and a half thousand copies. She was writing for that self-supporting coterie who read one another's work in the little magazines. Publication in the *New Yorker* widened her readership enormously, both at home and abroad. It is the most influential literary magazine in the world, precisely because it is not purely literary, but is a mass circulation magazine, covering the arts, current affairs and lifestyle issues. Munro's association with the *New Yorker* has continued. They have first refusal for her stories, many of them appearing in its pages ahead of the collections. This means that her identity as a Canadian author is complicated by affiliations with American writers.

The pressure to turn out a novel was considerable during the seventies. The form of *Who Do You Think You Are?*/*The Beggar Maid* went through many revisions, during composition and on its way to publication. It was dropped by one large American publisher, and eventually accepted by another. 'Simon's Luck' was added at a late stage, and some stories saved for the next collection, *The Moons of Jupiter* (1982). In their final state, both *The Beggar Maid* and *Lives of Girls and Women* are generic hybrids, combining features of the novel with those of short fiction and autobiography. The stories follow one another chronologically, and are linked by a central character, but they are also self-contained. Acceptance by the *New Yorker* gave Munro the freedom to experiment in this way, and it bestowed legitimacy on her choice of genre.

As Carver's testimony shows, the problems of combining an artistic vocation with day-to-day living are not unique to women; neither is the conflict between the writer's need for solitude and the desire for human contact, especially family life. But the sense of an acutely personal divide is a female dilemma, perhaps because those fluid ego boundaries that Choderow describes make it hard for women to compartmentalize their activities. It is difficult for those born since the women's liberation movement to imagine how absolute the choices were in the 1950s. Muriel Spark and Doris Lessing both gave up their children. Munro's experimentation with genre may be regarded, at least partially, as a response to these circumstances. With supportive agents and editors, she has been able to break through the barriers. During the 1980s, her reputation was consolidated by *The Moons of Jupiter* and *The Progress of Love*. Since then, new collections have appeared every four years or so, and her work has been translated into thirteen languages. Despite her own reservations, Munro has nothing left to prove. She has already answered the challenge, *Who Do You Think You Are?* Personal and artistic choices once regarded as limitations are now perceived as strengths, and her failures as her great success.

3

Epiphanies and Intuitions: The Short-Story Genre

One of the distinctive features of the short-story genre is its ability to engage with the passing moment. In the traditional novel, experience is cumulative. Characters evolve over time, and themes develop, moving towards resolution at the end. While there may be intercutting between past and present, events succeed one another in logical sequence. *Lives of Girls and Women* and *The Beggar Maid* adhere to this linear progression, in that each is a type of *Bildungsroman*, charting a life chronologically. But the individual stories do not together constitute a single plot; they do not follow a chain of events. Fragmenting her protagonists' lives into self-contained stories allows Munro to break free from a unified, centralized narrative, embracing what seems arbitrary and diffuse in subjective experience. Time is organized as a continuum, with no strict dividing line between past and present.

Each episode is constructed elliptically, shifting around in time and space. There is also a heightened awareness of the present moment, as each story seems to open and close randomly, in the middle of ongoing events. 'Simon's Luck' begins in the present tense, describing the adult Rose wandering about on Saturday nights, wishing she had invitations (*BM* 156). The story slips into the past tense, with the recollection of a party two years previously, where she began her disappointingly brief affair with Simon. The story ends 'a year or so later', that is, twelve months before the 'now' of the story, when Rose discovers, by chance, that he is dead. Throughout the story, we are reminded of transience – by Rose's Saturday night glimpses into lighted windows, or by her final meeting with a barely remembered acquaintance, who tells her the news about Simon.

At this stage in the collection, Rose is leading a nomadic existence as an actor and teacher. Earlier, in 'The Beggar Maid', Rose is a college student, being courted by the bourgeois Patrick. By the subsequent story, their marriage is already disintegrating. The abrupt transitions between stories accentuate the sense of personal dislocation. Rose's life does not run in a straight line. Throughout the collection, Rose travels back and forth, her journeys traversing ever greater distances. In 'Half a Grapefruit', 'Rose wrote the Entrance, she went across the bridge, she went to high school' (*BM* 41). As an outsider, from West Hanratty, she is attempting to join the middle-class 'towners'. In 'Wild Swans', her first unaccompanied train ride to Toronto is fraught with peril. Her stepmother Flo warns her to look out for White Slavers, and, in fact, she is molested by an elderly minister. The revulsion Rose feels during this encounter is mingled with curiosity, and with wonder at the spectacle beyond the train windows:

> Such cunning antics now, such popular visions. The gates and towers of the Exhibition Grounds came into view, the painted domes and pillar floated marvelously against her eyelids' rosy sky. Then flew apart again in celebration. (*BM* 65)

The orgasmic imagery and the wordplay are unmistakable. In the teenage Rose's ambivalent response, the one emotion that seems to be absent is shame, the feeling that haunts her elsewhere.

Rose's journey away from home is liberating. It allows her to change and re-invent her identity. She is always on the move. In her life, as for so many women over the last hundred years, continuity is fractured by increased social mobility, changes in gender roles and the breakdown of traditional family structures. Successive generations no longer duplicate each other; Flo's knowledge of life in the city is limited to the stories she tells about working, briefly, in a coffee shop at Union Station. The cultural distance from Hanratty widens with the journeys Rose makes to a college education and married life in the Vancouver suburbs.

Rose's geographical and social migration also brings a crippling instability. Education alienates Rose from her own background, but does not make her comfortable with Patrick's wealthy family in British Columbia. She has difficulty making herself a home anywhere, and in making permanent relationships. In 'Providence', Rose relocates to a town in the mountains. The story traces a complicated web of abortive itineraries and unsuccessful trips. Rose brings her daughter, Anna, back from the city, to live with her – an experiment which soon seems doomed to failure. She attempts a rendezvous with a lover from Calgary, who has other travel commitments involving Wisconsin and England. Her desperate negotiations when her plans are disrupted, first by illness then by bad weather, are prefigured in the story's opening. In the early days of the break-up, when Patrick and Rose are still in the same house, Anna keeps going to sleep in the marriage bed, where Patrick now sleeps alone. She is regularly carried back to her own bed. Everything is unsettled. Ordinary domestic arrangements demand enormous energy.

Reading 'Simon's Luck' is as exhausting as watching characters in a Chekhov play; like them, Rose is killing time with private rituals, placing her diminishing faith in a chimera. She thinks she has met 'the man for my life' (*BM* 168) and yet, despite the plans they make together, she never hears from him again. Her attempts to conjure him back by superstitious gestures, game-playing and guesswork only demonstrate her lack of control:

> Putting her hand into the mailbox and drawing the mail out without looking at it, refusing to leave the college until five o'clock, putting a cushion against the telephone to block her view of it; pretending inattention. Watch-pot thinking. (*BM* 171)

When Rose finds out what happened to Simon, she is filming a scene from a soap opera, in which a character threatens to throw herself off a ferry. Rose reflects that, although these cliffhangers are fairly common, they rarely result in the death of a major character. Television is more reassuring than lived experience. 'People watching trusted that they would be protected from predictable disasters, also from those shifts of emphasis that throw the story line open to question, the disarrangements which demand new judgements and solutions, and throw the windows open on inappropriate unforgettable scenery' (*BM* 177).

In 'Simon's Luck', events are governed by contingency, rather than individual choice or external logic. Simon's experience during the war has made him believe in lucky signs, but neither his destiny, nor Rose's, is quite so predictable. Rose observes that 'people's lives were surely more desperate than they used to be' (*BM* 171), because the old way of life is overthrown. Local farms are vanishing, people commute to factories and the church building is taken over by a strange new sect. Trapped by the unwritten rules laid down by the sexual revolution, Rose cannot bring herself to make direct contact with Simon. She simply assumes that he has lost interest. Her pain and frustrations prompt her to leave town, initially intending to play truant for time, and then following an instinct to hit the road again. In middle age, the urge to escape has become habitual:

> she thought how many letters she had written, how many overblown excuses she had found, having to leave a place, or being afraid to leave a place, on account of some man. Nobody knew the extent of her foolishness, friends who had known her twenty years didn't know half of the flights she had been on, the money she had spent, and the risks she had taken. (*BM* 173)

The journey onward stands for an open destiny. Rose is, in one sense, a picaresque figure, choosing freedom by embracing contingency. In another sense, she is repeating an endless cycle, motivated largely by the powerful sense of shame: 'The most mortifying thing of all was simply hope, which burrows so deceitfully at first, masks itself cunningly, but not for long'. The fact that her humiliation is entirely private does not ameliorate her suffering. Repeated humiliation has made her fatalistic; even if Simon does reappear, 'some morning she could wake up and she would know by his breathing that he was awake beside her and not touching her, and that she was not supposed to touch him' (*BM* 173).

Her anxieties focus on her own corporeality, as a lover's sexual desire mutates, inexorably, into repugnance: 'she would have to be ashamed of, burdened by, the whole physical fact of herself, the whole outspread naked digesting putrefying fact'. This apparent self-loathing is perhaps connected to the fear of exposing emotional need – 'so much female touching is asking ... women's tenderness is greedy'. (*BM* 173.) It may also be regarded as another example of shame's double edge. Rose is imagining herself into her lover's subjectivity. She is seeing herself through his disenchanted eyes, but those eyes are her invention. Perhaps we should reverse subject and object, turning his imagined gaze back on the spectator. The rejection of long-term intimacy then belongs to Rose, but is projected onto Simon's physical disgust.

The cyclical movements in Rose's life are reflected in a circular narrative structure, within the individual stories and the collection as a whole. Each instalment is situated in an unspecified present, which looks both backwards and forwards, containing time frames which overlap across the individual stories. The concluding stories, 'Spelling' and 'Who Do You Think You Are?', revisit Hanratty, juxtaposing childhood memories with Rose's adult self. By anticipating future events, the stories sometimes seem to share her fatalism; her marriage is described in the context of its dissolution. In the tellingly titled 'Providence', she feels that walking out on Patrick has always been inevitable: 'Even on her wedding day she had known this time would come, and that if it didn't she might as well be dead' (*BM* 138). Yet this intention has never been fully conscious:

> Even to say she had been planning to break, had started to break, was wrong, because she had done nothing at all intelligently, it had happened as painfully and ruinously as possible with all sorts of shilly-shallying and reconciling and berating, and right now she felt as if she was walking a swinging bridge and could only keep her eyes on the slats ahead, never look down or around.   (*BM* 138)

The fragmented, repetitive syntax in this long, wandering sentence speaks for doubt and hesitation. In retrospect, Rose's actions appear predetermined, but there is no clearly discernible agency behind them, beyond chance and coincidence. The ferry, on which Rose hears the news about Simon, might remind us of the imaginary bridge; Rose is permanently in transit.

The discovery that Simon was probably suffering from cancer during their affair shifts the scale of events, causing her to revise her solipsistic interpretation of his actions. While fatalism insists on a single, unbroken line between the separate compartments of past, present and future, this new version multiplies the possibilities. Past and present co-exist, each conditioning the other as we move towards the unforeseeable future.

The short story's affinity with the passing moment has been noted by theorists since Edgar Allan Poe. He insisted that 'all high excitements are necessarily transient', and that a short story, read in a single session, attained a 'unity of effect or impression' impossible in other literary forms.[1] It finds particular expression in the work of modernist writers, at the start of the twentieth century. Modernist concepts of time were inspired by the French philosopher, Bergson, who contrasted the immeasurable experience of 'real time' or 'duration' with the artificial, though socially necessary, imposition of 'clock time'. As duration, past and present intermingle: 'memory, inseparable in practice from perception, contracts into a single intuition many moments of duration'.[2] Such an intuition may be equated with the Joycean epiphany – a rare and fleeting revelation, transcending clock time and briefly uniting subjective reality with external objects. In Joyce's original formulation, it involves an empathic understanding of the true reality of the material world, so that 'the soul of the commonest object ... seems to us radiant'.[3] Virginia Woolf also speaks of spontaneously generated 'moments of being,'[4] which transform mundane experience through sensory impressions.

Modernist short fiction is more concerned with exploring internal states of consciousness than devising elaborate external plots. Narrative is constructed by the interaction of memories and perceptions, with the epiphany serving as its turning point. Stories by Joyce, Woolf or Mansfield resist closure, ending on an image, a question or a gesture. Munro's modernist predecessors developed a mode of storytelling which also shaped the work of later influences, such as Eudora Welty, Carson McCullers and Flannery O'Connor. She herself both renews and subverts these techniques. Following the modernist paradigm, she presents time as flux, rather than discrete succession. But while modernist writers try to grasp a fragmented and mobile reality, Munro uses the subjective experience of time as duration to suggest that we live within many, irreconcilable truths.

This can be demonstrated with a closer look at temporal indeterminacy in 'The Jack Randa Hotel'. From the very first paragraph, the narrative starts doubling back on itself:

> On the runway, in Honolulu, the plane loses speed, loses heart, falters and veers on the grass, and bumps to a stop A few yards it seems from the ocean. Inside, everybody laughs. First a hush, then the laugh. Gail laughed herself. Then there was a flurry of introductions all around. Beside Gail are Larry and Phyllis from Spokane. (*OS* 161)

'Gail laughed herself' takes the reader a tiny step backwards out of the present, in a passage which is packed with temporal and spatial disorientation. The first narrative, describing Gail's arrival in Honolulu, is interrupted by a second, taking the reader successively further into her past life, in Canada. We learn first about her habits after she separated from her lover, Will, and then about how they first met. Eventually, this backwards chronology is disrupted by smaller digressions, covering Gail's earlier history, and some of Will's. The present tense 'now' of Gail's journey gives way to a fragmented 'then', told in the past tense.

It is, however, a past without dates. 'Gail came to Walley one summer in the seventies' (*OS* 165) is as close as we come to an external chronology. Usually, the passage of time is marked internally, through emotional transitions: 'There came a time when just the tone of his voice, saying "Your shoelace is undone" as she went ahead of him on a walk – just that – could fill her with despair' (*OS* 167).

Past and present cross into one another, as the second narrative rejoins the first in Brisbane Airport. The purpose of Gail's journey is to follow Will and his new, younger partner to Australia. In his mailbox, she discovers one of his letters, marked return to sender. He has written to a woman whose surname in the phonebook is the same as his, hoping they might be related. She has since died. Gail writes back, pretending to be this 'Catherine Thornaby'. She also rents the woman's apartment, under another assumed name.

When Will finally guesses his correspondent's true identity, she heads back to Brisbane Airport. In a broadly circular gesture, the reader has been taken from one airport to another, and to an ending which is also the start of another journey. Just as the story begins in a moment of transition, part-way through Gail's journey to the Antipodes, so it ends on the cusp of an unpredictable future: *'Now it's up to you to follow me'* (*OS* 189). The circular structure and the open ending locate the story within the present moment, as it unfolds. The events in Australia are told chronologically, but their sequence is disrupted, not only by memories, but through the letters exchanged by Gail and Will. Letters are, in a sense, outside time, combining the moment of composition with that of reception, as well as the time evoked by their contents.

Towards the end of 'The Jack Randa Hotel', Will's note, *Gail, I know it's you* (*OS* 188), transmutes into what at first appears to be the live Will, speaking to her:

> *Gail, I know you're in there! I know you're there on the other side of the door.*
>
> *Gail! Galya!*
>
> *Talk to me, Gail. Answer me. I know you're in there.*
>
> *I can hear you. I can hear your heart beating through the keyhole and your stomach rumbling and your brain jumping up and down.*
>
> *I can smell you through the keyhole. You. Gail.* (*OS* 188)

Fee fi fo fum – is it really Will making this speech, or does Gail's hyperactive brain grant him the monstrous language of giants?

Munro frequently uses italics in this way, to foreground a key utterance. Italics usually denote quotation. In Munro, they often signal something more ambiguous – words which originate in some one else's speech, but have been absorbed into a character's consciousness. There is a very clear example in the repetition of *'Was there something you wanted?'* throughout 'Pictures of the Ice' (*Friend of My Youth*), which I discuss in the next chapter. In 'A Queer Streak' (*The Progress of Love*) the transition between quotation and inner speech is more complex. Violet's fiancé breaks off their engagement, fearing that her sister's apparent lunacy will compromise his standing as a minister. Desperately unhappy, she prays for some kind of

release. Her prayers are seemingly answered: 'Words settled
on her, and were like cool, cool cloths binding her' (*PL* 232).
She accepts what she now believes to be her true purpose in
life:

> To look after them. All of them, all of your family, and Dawn Rose in
> particular. To look after them all, and Dawn Rose in particular. (*PL*
> 232)

'*Look after them*' is divine revelation, wrapped inside Violet's
own head. It is up to the reader to decide how authentic the
oracle has been, as Dawn Rose recovers and eventually
marries, leaving Violet stuck on the farm. In 'The Jack Randa
Hotel', the ambiguity is taken further still. The true provenance
of the italicized speech attributed to Will cannot be resolved.
The repetitive phrases echo through the closing pages, as the
narrative becomes increasingly fragmented, and any sense of
an ordered reality begins to break down.

It is now evident that the events of Gail's journey are to be
read as possibilities, rather than established facts; the word
'can' changes from an auxiliary to a conditional verb.

> Words most wished for can change. Something can happen to
> them, while you are waiting. *Love – need – forgive. Love – need –
> forever.* The sound of such words can become a din, a battering, a
> sound of hammers in the street. And all you can do is run away,
> so as not to honor them out of habit. (*OS* 188)

In the airport shop, Gail buys a box made by Australian
aborigines, whose pattern reminds her of an experience she
shared with Will. Unlike the earlier, generalized account of
their relationship, this passage relates a single, unique instance:

> The yellow dots flung out in that way remind Gail of something
> she saw last fall. She and Will saw it. They went for a walk on a
> sunny afternoon. They walked from their house by the river up a
> wooded bank, and there they came on a display that they had
> heard about but never seen before.
> Hundreds, maybe thousands, of butterflies were hanging in the
> trees, resting before their long flight down the shore of Lake Huron
> and across Lake Erie, then on south to Mexico. They hung there
> like metal leaves, beaten gold – like flakes of gold tossed up and
> caught in the branches. (*OS* 189)

The rekindling of the past within the present through vivid sense impressions delivers what at first seems to be a textbook example of the modernist epiphany. When Gail sees the yellow pattern on the box, the interval between the present moment and the specific instance when she saw the butterflies is temporarily elided. In her own mind, that instance a year ago in Canada is taking place within the present moment, here in Brisbane airport. But the past can never be regained exactly as it was. As Bergson himself points out, 'the essence of time is that it goes by; time already gone by is the past, and we call the present the instant in which it goes by'.[5] Even as it arises, the sublime moment is squandered, undercut by Will's sarcasm:

> 'Like the shower of gold in the Bible,' Gail said.
> Will told her she was confusing Jove and Jehovah.   (*OS* 189)

Despite the brisk insistence that 'She and Will saw it', the couple are not united by the heightened awareness of an essential reality. Each is living their own story, now and then – which makes four stories altogether, including whatever version Will may have stored in his memory. As the unique instance recedes into the past, it is revised, according to hindsight. The epiphanic moment is re-oriented, in the context not only of Will's treachery, but also of his mother's disease:

> On that day, Cleata had already begun to die and Will had already met Sandy. This dream had already begun – Gail's journey and her deceits, then the words she imagined – believed – that she heard shouted through the door.
> *Love-forgive*
> *Love-forget*
> *Love-forever*
> Hammers in the street.   (*OS* 189)

Corporeal images pervade Munro's story – Gail's self-consciousness about her middle-aged body; the elderly neighbour who dies grasping her hand. Both mortality and the death of love are symptoms of mutability. Personal identity is the one thing that seems stable: 'she knows him at once, she will always know him, and will always have to call out to him when she sees him ...' (*OS* 187). But this too is inevitably subject to change, made palpable through the human body's gradual decline. We may experience time as boundless 'duration', but we are also reminded of its irresistible forward momentum, towards decay and death.

Joyce and Mansfield sometimes deliver a 'false' epiphany, where transcendence is frustrated. In Mansfield's story 'Bliss' (1918), the heroine, Bertha, undergoes what seems to be an endless moment of wordless communion with another woman as they gaze upon a pear tree. Later on, she glimpses a mysterious, but unmistakably compromising interchange between this new-found soul mate and her own husband, with whom she also believes she has achieved a fresh rapport. Like Joyce's 'The Dead' (*Dubliners*, 1914), Mansfield's story measures the void between our own subjective thoughts and the minds of others. However well we may think we know even those closest to us, their interior consciousness cannot be fathomed. We can only guess and, like Bertha, try to interpret.

Mansfield's story ends in confusion. The contradictions between Bertha's imaginings and the external world are left unresolved. Yet the ending also affirms the timeless, inviolate image of the pear tree:

> Bertha simply ran over to the long windows.
> 'Oh, what is going to happen now?' she cried.
> But the pear tree was as lovely as ever and as full of flower and as still.[5]

The epiphanic image stands for a scarcely expressible, essential reality, behind the perplexities of everyday life. This reality may be elusive, but it exists.

In Munro's work, the notion of conflicting subjective experience, explored by Mansfield, Joyce and others, destabilizes the possibility of any ultimate truth. The world now consists of numerous coexisting possibilities. Will's shouts are 'imagined', 'believed', within 'this dream', which began at some point that the reader cannot establish. It has become impossible to untangle fantasy from reality, or to pinpoint a moment when they might exchange. 'The Jack Randa Hotel' is full of crossed messages and misinformation. When Australians ask Gail what part of the States she hails from, she pretends to be first a Texan, and then from Oklahoma. Nothing is as it seems; even the title derives from a mishearing of 'jacaranda'. Ambiguities are never resolved, or contradictions reconciled.

In her *Meanjin* interview with Pleuke Boyce and Ron Smith, Munro characterizes *Open Secrets* as a collection which is especially concerned with parallel realities. Ideas of succession, she says, are imposed on our lives, even though we are always faced with several possibilities:

> We rarely live beyond the one reality we define or choose for ourselves. Yet things happen simultaneously in the universe. Something completely unimportant really does matter, at least in one version of the future. And rarely is it what we expect.

This is a shift in emphasis from the earlier work, but it is not an entirely new development. Most of her stories are multi-dimensional; competing narratives overlap, as events are reviewed from changing perspectives. The re-contextualizing which 'Simon's Luck' calls 'disarrangement' is manifested as Gail's new attitude towards the butterflies. Munro often uses autobiographical and historical forms of discourse to investigate inconsistencies in memory or conflicting accounts of the past. In *The Beggar Maid*, the fatalism induced by hindsight is challenged by contingency. If the future is unpredictable, it also contains several possibilities. By going down these imagined paths, *Open Secrets* extends Munro's explorations into multiple versions of the past into rival versions of present and future.

Gail's trip is open and uncircumscribed. She is merely disguised as a tourist, someone who is heading for a known destination. Her name suggests the restless movement both of weather and the galah birds she sees in Australia. The yellow-patterned box evokes the wanderings of the aboriginal people, and the spatially conceived 'storylines' which, like Munro's own work, resist closure. Munro's characters are perpetually on the move, disappearing, escaping or taking to the open road, and while they often return they are never really settled. Her stories also move back and forth through time.

They also compact time, like the packed graveyard in 'Hard-Luck Stories' – 'lives pressed down like layers of rotting fabric, disintegrating dark leaves' (*MJ* 196). Munro is fascinated by detritus, junk and jumble – for instance, the optometrist's equipment and the sunken car in 'The Love of a Good Woman', which I discuss in the next chapter. In the old houses she describes, converted into rural retreats or hippy communes, something from the past still just about endures. Past and present permeate one another, like those leaves. Stories which piece together family history – for instance, 'Chaddeleys and Flemings' in *The Moons of Jupiter* (1982) – make the doomed attempt to restore narrative continuity to the disintegrating past.

Time changes everything – even the dead – and the dynamics of change are intrinsic to language itself. The next chapter looks more closely at the diversity of voices in Munro's fiction, and at the part played by secrecy and silence.

4

Did You Tell? Speech, Silence and Double-Voiced Discourse

The interaction between past and present in Munro's fiction might be regarded as a kind of dialogue. This is a term used by Bakhtinian theory, to analyse the clash and interplay of different voices within a single text, and I have found it especially useful in getting to grips with the different layers of meaning in Munro's work. According to Bakhtin, dialogue is implicit within all forms of language. The words that we speak or write take their meanings in response to what has been said before, and in anticipation of what may follow. Prose fiction takes its strength from its ability to encompass all these different dimensions, and 'novelistic' discourse is by nature 'double-voiced'. Within every word, the speech of the characters mingles with an authorial voice. This is particularly evident in free indirect discourse, defined by Bakhtin as 'inner speech transmitted . . . by the author'.[1]

Free indirect discourse enables the author to slide in and out of a character's consciousness, maintaining an ironic distance that Munro exploits to the full in her 1990 collection, *Friend of My Youth*. All, except the title story, are told in the third person. In the title story itself, as in other confessional narratives, such as 'Hard-Luck Stories' in *The Moons of Jupiter* (1982), this ironic interplay is achieved by hindsight, as the narrator comments on her former self. In both kinds of narrative, competing voices are, in Bakhtinian terms, 'relativized' or 're-accentualized', accumulating fresh meanings relative to one another. No single voice is privileged, not even the author's, in the perpetual motion of verbal communication.

43

This becomes evident if we take a close look at Munro's 'Pictures of the Ice'.

'Pictures of the Ice' tells the story of Austin, a United Church minister who, a year after his wife's death from cancer, is apparently planning to remarry in Hawaii. Karin, who is cleaning out his house for him, discovers that he is in fact leaving for a distant part of Canada, where he drowns in a supposed accident. Here, Karin is remembering the break-up of her marriage after her husband's conversion to Christian fundamentalism:

> It didn't really surprise her that he got as mad at her now for drinking one beer and smoking one cigarette as he used to do when she wanted to stop partying and go to bed at two o'clock. He said he was giving her a week to decide. No more drinking, no more smoking, Christ as her saviour. One week. Karen said don't bother with the week. After Brent was gone, she quit smoking, she quit drinking, she also quit going to Austin's church. She gave up on nearly everything but a slow, smouldering grudge against Brent, which grew and grew. (*FMY* 145)

Syntactically, the first sentence belongs to the posited author, but the vocabulary and the emotional stance are Karin's. Superficially, 'don't bother with the week' needs only a change in punctuation to become direct speech; in fact, Karin's speech, and Karin's consciousness, merge seamlessly with the authorial voice.

What this passage suggests most of all is someone going over a conversation again and again – Karin nursing her grudge. The presence of the 'speaking person' is deeply ingrained in Munro's style, which often recalls small-town gossip. The swift movement between direct and free indirect discourse is typical of oral storytelling, and so is the fluidity of tenses ('After he hangs up, he says to Karin . . .', *FMY* 149).

As well as oral speech, double-voiced discourse incorporates parody, intertextuality and other forms of stylization. Here, 'Christ as her Saviour' imports the idiolect of the born-again Christian, while the repetition of 'quit' classifies religion within the language of addiction; thus, two competing types of language encounter one another within a single utterance. 'Quit' then develops into an authorial 'gave up', in the ambivalent context of 'gave up on nearly everything'.

Munro makes extensive use of what Bakhtin calls 'speech genres' – the familiar conventions appropriate to a particular context. Evangelical preaching, jokes, sales patter and talk about the weather are each based on shared rules, and are all dialogically interrelated within Munro's story. When registers clash, they often indicate social or ideological conflict. Karin writes 'Lazarus Sucks' on Brent's car (*FMY* 139). (Lazarus House is the religious hostel run by Brent.) Speaking to his daughter, Austin falls back on language more appropriate to a sermon than to family conversation: 'There's more than one way to love God, and taking pleasure in the world is surely one of them. That's a revelation that's come to me rather late' (*FMY* 145).

Austin is talking on the telephone, which, along with the answering machine, brings its own set of conventions. By borrowing conventions from all these different 'genres', Munro varies the texture of the writing. She also exploits the sense of dislocation inherent within telephone conversation where the speakers are simultaneously present and absent. Although Austin's nominal interlocutor is his daughter in Montreal, his words are actually read in counterpoint to Karin's silent speculations, as she eavesdrops. These speculations continue, unspoken, when Megan rings again to talk to Karin. Because the story is focalized through Karin, the reader never hears both sides of Austin's phone calls. Within the text, Karin's mute participation dominates the family discussions, creating fantasy images shared by the reader ('Wouldn't her voice bring such looks to mind even if you'd never seen her?' *FMY* 147). Although both Austin and Megan are talkers rather than listeners, their speech cannot be other than anticipation and response ('I know I'm behaving just the way adult children are supposed to behave' *FMY* 147).

The interaction of different types of language is fundamental both to the style and content of Munro's work. The use of speech genres highlights formulaic types of communication which may conceal the speaker's emotions, even when they are not telling out-and-out lies. Free indirect discourse reveals what is thought but never spoken out loud; Austin's lies about a marriage in Hawaii are mirrored by Karin's strategic silences.

Cora Kaplan has observed that patriarchal cultures prefer women to be silent, and that female access to public discourse is restricted.[2] In 'Pictures of the Ice', Austin points out that his son's phone calls about his marriage plans concentrate on his financial situation, while his daughter discusses his mental state – conventionally male and female anxieties, centring on, respectively, the material and the personal. As his own conversation indicates, he conceals his private thoughts behind public speech genres associated with masculinity. This is signalled at the beginning of the story, when he acquiesces with an offensive joke in a men's-wear store, notwithstanding his personal distaste.

Karin seeks empowerment through silence – not only by keeping Austin's secret, but also by withholding speech during crises in her marriage. After the marriage breaks down, she takes private speech into a public context by airing a 'public grudge against her ex-husband' (FMY 139). She interrupts other people's conversations and scrawls abuse on Brent's car, transgressing conventionally female speaking positions. Yet, like Karin's pilfering from Austin's house, these speech acts are essentially subversive, rather than proactive. The message on the car is, at least theoretically, anonymous and temporary; she writes it in the dust. Karin is turning female silence and a restricted public role to her own advantage. Austin's own concealments parallel those strategies. As a fragile, elderly man, whose patriarchal role in the church has been usurped by Brent, he has lost the power to exert male authority. He resorts to strategies based on silence and subterfuge, which are conventionally encoded within the feminine.

'Pictures of the Ice' is typical of Munro's fiction, in its use of parody and the grotesque, jokes and puns like the wordplay on 'bizarre', a term which Austin's daughter, Megan, applies to his behaviour:

'Lets face it, Karin. Mother was a snob.' (Yes, she is drunk.) 'Well, she had to have something. Dragged around from one dump to another, always doing good. Doing good wasn't her thing at all. So now, *now*, he gives it all up, he's off to the easy life. In Hawaii! Isn't it bizarre?' (FMY 147)

Karin associates 'bizarre' with teenage slang on television; Megan's use of the word suggests her emotional immaturity (she is 'around thirty' on page 145). The connotations of 'bizarre' are widened further by the homophonous 'bazaar', which reminds Karin of church fêtes:

> Then she thinks of Megan's mother on the chintz-covered sofa in the living room, weak and yellow after her chemotherapy, one of those padded, perky kerchiefs round her nearly bald head. Still, she could look up at Karin with a faint, formal surprise when Karin came into the room. 'Was there something you wanted, Karin?' The things that Karin was supposed to ask her, she would ask Karin.
>
> *Bizarre. Bazaar. Snob.* (FMY 147–8)

Karin's musing are followed by more from Megan's phone call, in which teenage slang is parodied again: 'We're talking about whether my father is sane or whether he has flipped his *wig*, Karin!' (FMY 148). The word 'wig' is dialogically related to the image of the kerchief round her dying mother's 'nearly bald head'. It also aptly evokes disguise; Austin is in fact, as Karin intuits, 'slipping out from under, fooling them, enjoying it' (FMY 154).

Munro's use of parody and wordplay may be further understood through another Bakhtinian concept, that of 'carnival ambivalence'. In popular tradition, carnival disrupts authority's efforts to impose a monolithic culture. It suspends all rules and hierarchies, delighting in the grotesque and celebrating bodily functions. Carnival time is cyclical. Birth and death, comedy and tragedy, are not opposed to one another; they are inseparable.

By extension, literature which imports carnival elements also subverts official culture, disrupting unitary meaning. While the jokes and wordplay all contribute to this ambivalence, it is Munro's representations of the body that offer the most striking examples of the carnivalesque.

Even as he prepares for his fake wedding, Austin is disintegrating physically:

> That downward slide is what's noticeable on him everywhere – face slipping down into neck wattles, chest emptied out and moulded into that abrupt, queer little belly. The flow has left dry channels, deep lines. Yet Austin speaks – it's his perversity to speak – as if out of a body that is light and ready and a pleasure to carry around. (FMY 146)

47

This body is almost – but not quite – a landscape. The disembodied voice suggests dismemberment. Above all, the grotesque body is a body which is never entirely completed, but is always being created and creating, in endless metamorphosis. We may be reminded here of the 'Gothic Mother' in 'The Peace of Utrecht' (*DHS* 200).

The reconciliation between birth and death is figured in the photographs Karin is left with after Austin's disappearance. In these pictures of frozen waves at a nearby lake, the invisible photographer is paradoxically a presence, 'blank in them, but bright' (*FMY* 155). The disappearance is implicated in the seasonal cycle of death and renewal: 'He has vanished as completely as the ice, unless the body washes up in the spring.' Whether or not his death is intentional, it represents escape from under the noses of his family and neighbours, 'slipping out from under, fooling them' (*FMY* 154). He has played the jester. Carnival laughter overturns social rules, and overcomes the fear of death.

Karin sends the photographs, anonymously, to Austin's children and to Brent:

> She doesn't write anything on the pictures or enclose any note. She won't be bothering any of these people again. The fact is, it won't be long till she'll be leaving here.
> She just wants to make them wonder. (*FMY* 155)

Munro exploits the internal dialogism of 'wonder', which implies both questioning and admiration. The recipients will wonder what the photographs are, who sent them and why. They may also wonder at the phenomenon of the strange, gigantic shapes. Austin's death is a 'wonder', a carnival show. Finally, the reader is also left 'wondering' at the story's unresolved ending.

Munro's stories often set riddles for the reader, by withholding information or by posing questions without answer; at the end of 'The Jack Randa Hotel', Gail is posing a riddle for Will. Her characters' reliance on subterfuge is paralleled by an elliptical narrative structure, in which the evidence is suppressed or dispersed. 'Pictures of the Ice' begins proleptically, teasing the reader with the enigma of sudden death:

> Three weeks before he died – drowned in a boating accident in a
> lake whose name nobody had heard him mention – Austin Cobbett
> stood deep in the clasp of a three-way mirror in Crawford's Men's
> Wear in Logan, looking at himself in a burgundy sports shirt and
> a pair of cream, brown and burgundy plaid pants. (*FMY* 137)

In fact, the brief summary between the dashes is the most
precise account of the actual circumstances of Austin's death
in the entire story. Similarly, a key event from Karin's past, the
death of her baby, is described almost parenthetically, three
quarters through the text. The bereavement is important, since
it both anticipates Austin's death and clarifies Karin's emotional state. She is paired with Austin, in her state of loss; they
are tacitly complicit in his escape, which foreshadows her own.

Constance Rooke attributes a tendency to tell 'truth at a
slant' in fiction by Munro and other Canadian women writers
to 'woman's long experience of indirection and introspection
and the need to consider the feelings of others'.[3] The titles of
two Munro collections, twenty years apart from one another,
evoke the interplay between speech and silence – *Something
I've Been Meaning to Tell You* (1974) and *Open Secrets* (1994).
Silence is as deeply embedded in the dialogic process as the
spoken word. Indeed, they are mutually dependent; gossip
cannot exist without secrecy.

Gossip is, allegedly, a female activity. Other types of
discourse are less available to women. Kaplan notes a 'sanction
against female obscenity',[4] limiting access to broad humour.
Munro combines an exploration of strategic silences in the
domestic sphere with carnival ambivalence. She is thus both
appropriating these silences and breaking a taboo against
female vulgarity. This is why Redekop calls her a 'female
clown',[5] likening her work to a circus parade.

But, while silence may often be a female strategy, it is not an
exclusively female prerogative. Although Munro's work is
written from an avowedly female perspective, and is deeply
implicated in the maternal, this does not mean that she has
nothing to say about men's lives. Prompted by her father's
death, 'The Moons of Jupiter', looks sympathetically at male
forms of discourse. In hospital, seriously ill with heart failure,
the narrator's father faces the prospect of his own demise by
analysing the phenomenon of near-death experience. He

spends the last visit from his daughter before a dangerous operation painstakingly naming all of Jupiter's moons. This assembling of factual information is a conventionally male attribute, and it will already be familiar to readers who remember Uncle Craig's unfinished history in *Lives of Girls and Women*. But while the information, once retrieved, is ordered systematically, there is a random element to its retention in memory. Like many of us, the father racks his brains for a word that's slipped his mind – '*shore*-less seas' (*MJ* 225), completing lines from a poem he probably recited at school. The image of Columbus on the brink of the unknown world is sadly apposite. Yet searching for the right word has also been a puzzle, a brainteaser. The answer could easily have been either of the alternatives he hit upon – either 'lonely' or 'empty'. For someone with little formal education, knowledge is arbitrary, retained haphazardly from schooldays or from newspapers or radio or whatever happens to be in the library. Yet his musings on memory may also have a relevance for the creative process:

> 'I was on the right track but I couldn't get it. But there now when you came into the room and I wasn't thinking about it all, the word popped into my head. That's always the way, isn't it?'   (*MJ* 225)

Talking about preparing to write, in her *Paris Review* interview, Munro says, 'The whole process might take about a week, the time of trying to think it through, trying to retrieve it, then giving it up and thinking about something else and then getting it back, usually quite unexpectedly, when I'm in the grocery store or out for a drive.'

The invisible connections that he likens to the workings of a computer may also be compared to the interconnections within the story itself; like the rest of Munro's work, 'The Moons of Jupiter' is structured by associations, rather than by linear causality. The father's fact-finding is part of a playful attitude to life, an interest in puzzles, jokes and games. Nothing, not even death, must be taken seriously. But the listing and the naming also recall James Agee's curatorial approach to representation, and the sufficiency of the material world. Like Grace Paley's 'A Conversation with my Father',[6] 'The Moons of Jupiter' uses dialogue with a dying father to reflect on the nature of storytelling and, in particular, the relationship between recording external reality and grasping subjective experience. The paternal influence on Munro's aesthetic – including its carnival aspects – should not be underestimated. She herself has said that she shares her father's 'angle of vision' (*PR* 240).

In both 'The Moons of Jupiter' and 'Pictures of the Ice', a woman plays along with a male preference for public, over private, forms of discourse. Complicity between the sexes has been a key theme in Munro's work. In 'Images' (*Dance of the Happy Shades*), a young girl is taught secrecy by her father when he takes her to look at his traps. She is being let into a violent male world, from which women are usually excluded. Her glimpses of a dead muskrat prefigure the meeting with a frightening, almost feral character, carrying an axe. Paranoid and reclusive, Joe nonetheless invites his acquaintance, Ben Jordan, and his daughter into his primitive underground house. Afterwards, Ben coaches his daughter not to mention the axe to her mother or her nurse, in case they are frightened: 'You and me aren't, but they might be' (*DHS* 42). Although she is repelled by the smelly, dirty cellar, and by Joe, this hidden male world is also potent and compelling. The episode is told as a memory, framed by her re-acquaintance with the nurse, Mary McQuade, whom she pretends not to recognize. She has learnt how to use subterfuge.

Munro returns to female collusion with male silence in the title story of *The Love of a Good Woman* (1998). The story opens and ends with yet more examples of Munro's unsolved riddles. We begin with the drowning of the optometrist, Dr Willens, in 1951, memorialized by his instruments on display in the local museum. We end with the undisclosed fate of Enid, a nurse who is literally flirting with danger on a lake nearby. Following a short introduction, this very long story divides into two self-contained narratives. The first, 'Jutland', details the reactions of the boys who find Willens's submerged car, with his body trapped inside. The second is split between three more numbered sections, 'Heart Failure', 'Mistake' and 'Lies'. It describes a difficult and protracted case for Enid, and her increasing attachment to her dying patient's family. The two strands at first seem unrelated; then, just before her death,

51

Jeanette Quinn[7] gives a lurid account of Willens's murder, at the hands of her jealous husband, Rupert. Once again, Munro uses narrative structure to baffle the reader, this time by delaying the second narrative's intersection with the first. The painstakingly detailed descriptions of the boys' family circumstances, in the first half of the story, seem irrelevant when these characters are jettisoned, in favour of an equally thorough account of how Enid turned to home nursing.

Again, as in 'Pictures of the Ice', narrative technique mirrors the characters' circumspection. Just as the boys put off telling anyone about what they have found, so the narrative procrastinates, by adding surplus information and introducing a second series of events. This apparently extraneous information camouflages whatever clues to Willens's death and Enid's fate lie in the text. Seen from Enid's perspective, Mrs Quinn is deranged, her story a malicious fantasy discharged from a disintegrating body. Yet its telling is sufficiently graphic to raise doubts in both Enid and the reader's mind. The minor mystery concerning the anonymous donor, who gave Willens's instruments to the Walley museum, offers a proleptic key to the deeper mysteries at the story's ending, if we connect them to Enid's plans for sorting out Rupert's home, 'saving and labelling' some of its contents:

> A house like this, lived in by one family for so long a time, and neglected for the past several years, would have plenty of bins, drawers, shelves, suitcases, trunks, crawl spaces full of things that it would be up to Enid to sort out, saving and labelling some, restoring some to use, send others by the boxload to the dump. When she got that chance she wouldn't balk at it. She would make this house into a place that had no secrets from her and where all order was as she had decreed. (*TLGW* 77)

Enid is the one of several conniving nurses in Alice Munro's fiction – Audrey Atkinson in 'Friend of My Youth', Mary McQuade in 'Images' – who insinuate themselves with their patients' relatives, taking charge where there is disorder and imposing a more rational, up-to-date lifestyle on the families they have colonized. Unlike Mary and Audrey, Enid is assigned an inner life. We share her perspective, rather than seeing her as an alien being, focalized through a narrator.

After Mrs Quinn's death, Enid takes a gamble. She arranges a scenario, on a boat in the middle of a lake, where, if Rupert is a murderer, he could get rid of her. There, she will test his reactions, when she repeats his dead wife's accusation:

> The different possibility was coming closer to her, and all she needed to do was to keep quiet and let it come. Through her silence, her collaboration in a silence, what benefits could bloom. For others, and for herself. (*TLGW* 75–6)

The verbs are conditional, looking towards the future. Nothing has yet happened; everything is anticipated. The story reaches its ultimate aporia, at dusk, with the boat 'waiting, riding in the shadows'. There is no telling if Enid is playing out a masochistic fantasy or taking a bold initiative. The closing passage balances light and dark, disorder and control: 'But if she concentrated on the motion of the boat, a slight and secretive motion, she could feel as if everything for a long way around had gone quiet'. (*TLGW* 78)

Enid regards Mrs Quinn's outburst as the last, random expulsion of a dying woman's energy. But perhaps it has also been triggered by her own implacable calm. The details of sexual molestation, violence and the disposal of a body are told with sardonic relish; the married woman aims to shock the spinster, whose familiarity with physiological degradation does not make her less of a prude. Once Jeanette Quinn has died, Enid's job is finished and she is expelled from a home to which she can lay no explicit claim. She has been ousted from her maternal role with the Quinn children by the intervention of Rupert's married sister. Like the governess in a gothic romance, she is expendable.

But Enid harnesses the capacity for silence induced by marginality to win self-empowerment. She resorts to the classically female tactics of manipulation, to get her man. The particular strategy that she is going to use on the lake takes a number of pages to develop as she decides her attitude towards Jeanette's story. Enid's rereading of this story is juxtaposed with a hazy memory from early childhood. Enid told her mother that she had seen her father in his office suckling a woman's breast; her mother persuaded her that she must have been dreaming. What this digression suggests is that it is pointless to seek truth or falsehood in Mrs Quinn's accusations. Enid has realized that we can select our own reality, suppressing whatever is better ignored:

> This was what most people knew. A simple thing that it had taken her so long to understand. This was how to keep the world habitable. (*TLGW* 76)

Tidying a physical space – saving, restoring, labelling or rejecting – acts as a metaphor for mental readjustment: 'she would make this house into a place that had no secrets from her and where all order was as she had decreed'. Enid has accepted that other people, the grown-ups, run their lives pragmatically. Her original plan, to provoke Rupert into either turning himself in or killing her, now seems like 'childish' desperation. (*TLGW* 77)

Rupert's attractions for Enid are complex. He is the strong, silent type – a dark, saturnine lover in the gothic tradition. But he also provides domesticity, complete with a ready-made family. The opportunity to entertain his motherless children enables Enid to identify with them, and ultimately to regress to an infantile state. When Mrs Quinn is on her deathbed, she asks the children what should happen when some one misbehaves:

> 'Now what if it was a very bad thing but nobody knew they did it? Should they tell that they did and be punished?' (*TLGW* 66)

Adults often adopt this sanctimonious, childlike discourse, using questions to manoeuvre children into a predetermined moral stance. These are the tactics used by Enid's mother, to dismiss the 'dream'. But even as she acts out her adult role, Enid is entering a personal dialogue, sounding out the children for her own reassurance, while pretending to be laying down the law. She concludes that 'If you do something very bad and you are not punished you feel worse, far worse, than if you are' (*TLGW* 66). This is conventional wisdom. What she will later realize is that it is a lie. Adults' lives do not conform to this simple morality. Who exactly, in the story, should be punished? Rupert? The children? Jeanette, for telling tales? Or Enid herself? (Carol L. Beran argues that she hastens Jeanette's death.[8])

Enid's passage into adult awareness brings us back to the story's opening section. The discourse of childhood permeates the whole story, from the beginning, when the museum's language, a dispassionate authorial voice and childish fancy combine to describe Willens's instruments. The ophthalmoscope is compared to a snowman; the retinoscope contains 'something like an elf's head' (*TLGW* 4). The boys believe that the place where they discover the body is called Jutland because of the planks that jut out of the river and the shore.

Enid and Rupert were originally schoolmates. She remembers herself and the other girls taunting him with the sound of his name – 'Hello, Rupert. Hello, Ru-pert' (*TLGW* 33). Rupert's ordeal is not unlike the teasing Bud, one of the boys who discovers Willens, gets from his sister in 'Jutland'. This parodic tone, the voice of the female bully, recurs in the language Mrs Quinn uses with Enid; being rude to her nurse is the only power she has left. The subsection called 'Mistake' is full of childish verbs like 'bang', 'wallop', 'bash'; and nouns like 'thing' and 'stuff'. Sex with Willens is a particularly lecherous version of 'doctors and nurses': 'It was like the same game every time, and she wasn't supposed to suspect what was going on, and when he had the thing out looking in her eye he wanted her to keep her panties on, him the dirty old cuss puffing away getting his fingers slicked in and puffing away' (*TLGW* 62). Enid is not 'playing' nurses – she is a real one – but she is perhaps playing house, when she takes over the Quinn family. Images of play-acting in *The Love of a Good Woman*, as a collection, recall the theatrical themes in *The Beggar Maid*, but with an added emphasis on the disjunction between adult and childhood roles. In 'The Children Stay', Pauline's involvement in amateur dramatics is paralleled by her husband's tireless 'parade of jokes and antics' (*TLGW* 193). In 'Rich as Stink' a child's penchant for dressing up in adult costumes leads to a dreadful accident.

'Jutland' expands Munro's interest in adolescence from the female experiences she has dealt with elsewhere into the self-enclosed world of a gang of boys, who roam around the deserted settlement on the riverbank. Although they talk together in what is almost a private language, they rarely communicate decisions verbally. Their way of avoiding trouble is to stay quiet when they run into adults, back in town – literally keeping their heads down. It therefore seems natural not to mention their discovery at home. Meeting up again after dinner, they hardly need to ask each other 'Did you tell?' (*TLGW* 22). When they come across the elderly special constable dozing under a tree, they start to spill the news. But in the time it takes for him to find his hearing aid, it is Cece, possibly the most responsible of the boys, who turns the whole thing into another tease, telling the policeman his flies are undone, so that all of them then run away. Eventually Bud spills the news to his mother, in a brief, almost parenthetic coda.

The 'Jutland' section, with all the details of the boys' family lives and their own private culture, exposes the gap between adult and childhood realities. It is while Captain Tervitt is girding himself up for civic duty, telling the boys first to hush and then to proceed, that they suddenly decide to subvert the power relationship. The boys resist adult authority and establish group autonomy through silence. The two separate narratives, the boys' story and Enid's, are in fact linked by the conflicting realms of child and adult, and by the different types of discourse generated by these different realities. Once again, shame is a powerful motivator. The children know that teasing is their best weapon available. For the dying Jeanette Quinn, humiliated by her deteriorating body, hectoring and embarrassing Enid is a means of deflecting her own shame.

By not immediately reporting their discovery, the boys are postponing adult intrusion into their autonomous world. Adults and children lead double lives; they each inhabit secret worlds, separate from those few experiences they share. This doubling is especially pronounced in men, because, like Ben Jordan in 'Images', they can compartmentalize work and home.

Rupert is taciturn. Arriving home late at nights, he asks Enid what she's been writing in her diary, but he says nothing about his own day, and does not respond directly to her news. Enid intuits his thoughts, believing that he likes to hear about her recording his children's sayings, but that he is unable to articulate that pleasure. A quiet intimacy develops between them over the newspaper crossword.

For the female listener, male silence confers mystique. Rupert's utterances, limited as they are to the purely functional – 'The oars are hid' (*TLGW* 78) – are charged with covert meaning. Carrying a hatchet to clear the path, on their way to the lake, he may remind the reader of Joe carrying his axe in 'Images'. The sinister aura around Joe and Rupert is merely an intensification of the thrill and the repulsion that the child feels, simultaneously, when she is out with her father, in his secret, brutal world. As they walk along the river, 'Images' describes a mysterious landscape in which she easily loses her sense of direction. The river keeps its own secrets: 'the noise the river made was not loud but deep, and seemed to come from away down in the middle of it, some hidden place where the water issued with a roar from underground' (*DHS* 37). Munro describes a river's 'hidden places' elsewhere – 'the deep holes, ominous beckoning places' in 'Everything Here Is Touchable and Mysterious'. The dark, riverside landscape in 'Images' distorts and misleads. It is also highly seductive.

5

Turning Points

In 'The Love of a Good Woman', two separate narratives are conjoined – Enid's story, and that of the boys who find Willens's body. The story is also subdivided into numbered chapters. 'Jutland' covers the day the corpse was discovered, while the rest of the story is split between three more sections, moving across a longer period. Each bears a title, rather like the display card attached to the optometrist's instruments in the museum. The label helps to order and categorize the material, but in itself it tell us very little; as James Agee said, 'description is a word to suspect'.[1] The cryptic titles – 'Heart Failure', 'Mistake', 'Lies' – recall the visual arts, perhaps abstract painting or photography. They are metonymic, using a fragmentary detail to stand for the whole.

There are many other breaks in the narrative, besides those indicated by the titles. Marked by white space or asterisks, they often indicate a shift in time. As we have seen in earlier chapters, these intricate elliptical patterns disrupt chronological succession. We read across the text, relating individual sections to one another, as if they were pictures at an exhibition; or, to use Munro's analogy, as if we were roaming back and forth between the rooms of a house. As the previous chapter argues, the childish 'spaces' introduced in 'Jutland' are revisited in the second half of the story, which is itself a whole labyrinth of interconnections. The enclosed space where Enid catechizes the children (*TLGW* 66) responds to Mrs Quinn's tale in 'Mistake', while simultaneously foreshadowing the 'dream' about her father's transgression (*TLGW* 74–5). The passage about the 'dream', in turn, suggests another reading of 'Mistake'; the very word 'dream' prompts a re-evaluation of

Enid's previous 'ugly dreams ... unlike any dreams she had ever had before' (*TLGW* 51). The permutations are infinite. Every utterance, whether a single word, or a whole 'chapter', like 'Mistake', is constantly re-accentualized in a changing context.

Linear storytelling leads the reader towards final resolution. One of the pleasures of reading is this sense of closure, for instance in crime fiction, when the mystery is solved and wrongdoers brought to justice. In Munro's work, this satisfaction is withheld. The crime is not wrapped up. The perpetrators are rarely punished, or even fully identified. 'Fits' (*The Progress of Love*) opens with a carefully observational passage, which might almost be a forensic report:

> The two people who died were in their early sixties. They were both tall and well built, and carried a few pounds of extra weight. (*PL* 106)

This is a conventional beginning, in terms of crime fiction. Deaths have occurred. The known facts are given, in a detached, pared-down style. Attention is gradually turned from the murdered couple to another couple, their neighbours, Peg and Robert. It is Peg who discovers the bodies, through a chain of petty circumstance, concerning the delivery of some eggs. The rest of the story concentrates on the witness, rather than victims or perpetrators. The police are duly notified, although, as in 'The Love of a Good Woman', we do not hear what they are told. Naturally, in a small town, the murder–suicide becomes the main topic of conversation. But Peg does not join in the gossip or discuss what she has seen with her family. Much of the narrative is focalized through her husband Robert, as he watches Peg quietly going about her business. They have married fairly recently, in middle age, and, like the couples in Carver's fiction, are both intimate and strange to one another.

While the dramatic events in 'Fits' are elided, the story is packed with the minutiae of everyday life. Local gossip is greedy for any mundane fact about the dead couple, the Weebles; while Peg and Robert's ongoing domestic routine is catalogued for the reader. When Robert encourages Peg to open up to him, she supplies one or two poignant details, especially the sight of a leg stretched out in the hallway. She does not mention something far more terrible, that he has learnt about from the police – Walter Weeble's shattered head, blasted out onto the landing:

> Not a leg. Not the indicative leg, whole and decent in its trousers, the shod foot. That was not what anybody turning at the top of the stairs would see and would have to step over, step through, in order to go into the bedroom and look at the rest of what was there. (*PL* 131)

Peg has faced the unimaginable. The sudden violence between another ordinary couple has disturbed Robert's security in his own marriage. Peg's inability, or refusal, to share the horror with him shows how remote they really are from one another. It is a comment upon their relationship; more generally, it draws attention to the difficulty of ever understanding what goes on in someone else's mind.

When unexplained deaths occur in Munro's fiction, the focus is often on the witness, rather than the perpetrator, and on their subjective response, rather than plot resolution. In 'Cortes Island' (*The Love of a Good Woman*), the young narrator takes on a job reading to her landlord's husband, who is barely able to communicate, following a stroke. He manoeuvres her towards an old newspaper article, which suggests his involvement with a suspicious death many years ago. Like Mrs Quinn, in 'The Love of a Good Woman', Mr Gorrie provokes perverse dreams in his carer. In these dream activities, the safe barrier between the transgressor and the 'normal' self is crossed. The dreamer is no longer a passive witness. She is implicated. (Although Enid's dreams precede the confession, they follow Jeanette Quinn's hints about Mr Willens.)

In Munro's work, sudden deaths provide 'disarrangements', disrupting routine patterns, and challenging previous assumptions. They are aspects of contingency, fluke events with unpredictable consequences for onlookers and survivors. In 'Accident' (*The Moons of Jupiter*), adulterous sex is interrupted by news of a child's death. But, far from ending the affair, the bereavement unexpectedly transforms it into a marriage. When the circumstances are suspicious, another dimension is added to the story, in the attempt to reconstruct the death and solve the mystery.

In *Open Secrets* (1994), both the title story and 'A Wilderness Station' are murder stories. Yet, in neither story can we be absolutely sure that a murder has taken place – or even a death, in 'Open Secrets', where a young girl goes missing on a hiking trip. 'Open Secrets' begins, like many crime stories, by emphasizing the element of chance: ' "And they almost didn't even go," Frances said' (*OS* 129). A sequence of mundane events is charged with retrospective meaning only because they culminated in a dramatic incident. The annual Canadian Girls In Training hike was almost rained off; hardly anyone was all that keen to go in any case. But they did go; the die was cast. As in a more conventional story, suspense is created, as we await the irrevocable outcome of seemingly unexceptional circumstances.

Crime fiction invites the reader to find the causal link which transforms this ordinary sequence. It fills in textual gaps, in order to recreate the pattern underlying an arbitrary arrangement of events. Ultimately, it asks whether a violent death has become inevitable, or whether it was produced by a random aberration. But while conventional crime writers restore unity, Munro uses Heather Bell's disappearance to generate further mysteries.

Heather Bell vanishes without trace. Local people speculate; she may have drowned or she could have run away. A farming couple approach a retired lawyer with their suspicions about a local eccentric, but police investigations find nothing to link Mr Siddicup to any abduction. Eventually, people lose interest, although rumours persist for a while.

The narrative is pieced together from local gossip, a ballad about Heather Bell, and the viewpoints of several individual characters – most particularly Maureen, the lawyer's wife. To borrow Bakhtin's comment on Dostoevsky, Munro's style contains 'a plurality of independent and unmerged voices and consciousnesses, a genuine polyphony of fully valid voices'.[2] All of these voices, including the authorial voice, have the same worth. They often conflict with each another. There is no supreme authorial consciousness offering a definitive judgement.

The story is told mostly through Maureen, as she reconstructs a drama long since spent. Her memories and suppositions mingle imperceptibly with voices drawn from hearsay or from oral testimony. Like Enid, Maureen serves as the audience for an accusation; Marian Hubbert's longwinded version of her encounter with Mr Siddicup (*OS* 144–51) is mediated by Maureen's consciousness, just as Mrs Quinn's confession is filtered through Enid's. And again, the accusation is re-examined subsequently. Maureen watches the couple resting on a wall, thinking themselves unobserved once they have left Lawyer Stephens's house. Marian removes the feathered hat she's been wearing for the occasion. Her husband settles it in his lap, stroking it tenderly 'as if he were pacifying a little scared hen' (*OS* 153). Marian stops him, taking charge 'the way a mother might interrupt the carrying-on of a simple-minded child – with a burst of abhorrence, a moment's break in her tired-out love' (*OS* 153–4). For Maureen, the moment is electrifying. But what has been revealed is never made explicit, and does not lead to further action. The narrative makes an apparent digression into Maureen's relationship with her elderly husband.

'Open Secrets' is less concerned with the fate of Heather Bell than with the subjective impact of her disappearance, both on the community and, especially, on Maureen. Thematic patterns emerge within the diffuse narrative structure, concerning male violence and female complicity, sexual guilt and the transition between childhood and adult subjectivity. But these patterns are irregular. They are based on a shifting dynamic, rather than on the search for uniformity. Lawyer Stephens is fulfilling the Willens role of dirty old man; the stroke which has slurred his speech has also unloosened an uncharacteristically sadistic sexual appetite. Marian's name echoes Maureen's. Both women's marriages have been regarded as opportunistic. Maureen married her boss; Theo got Marian's farm. But, although Theo may leave the talking to Marian, his speech is not physically impaired; it is the man she accuses, Mr Siddicup, who has lost his voice, following throat surgery.

Both women cover up for their men, repressing a secret disgust. But while Marian, like Enid, exerts a quasi-maternal control, Maureen, in her middle-class marriage, is far less empowered. She has not made a full transition from Lawyer Stephens's office to her home; she is still the Jewel (*OS* 138).

Her position has been exacerbated by infertility, following a miscarriage. Childlessness leaves her stranded between adolescence and adulthood:

> Having children changed you. It gave you the necessary stake in being grown-up, so that certain parts of you – old parts – could be altogether eliminated and abandoned. Jobs, marriage didn't quite do it – just made you *act* as if you'd forgotten them.   (*OS* 132)

Heather Bell's disappearance activates Maureen's memories of her own teenage misbehaviour at camp, smoking, making fun of Miss Johnstone and playing 'Truth or Dare', which also involves talking and behaving 'dirty' – 'take off your pajama top and show your boobs; eat a cigarette butt; swallow dirt . . . go and pee in front of Miss Johnstone's tent' (*OS* 139). Maureen remembers herself as 'a shrieker, a dare-taker' (*OS* 139), someone who indulges in the 'rude language' that induces 'the proper motherly kind of fit' in her adult peers (*OS* 132). Now it is her husband who is noisy, during sex; she is afraid of being heard.

In the interval between Maureen's miscarriage and the stroke, Lawyer Stephens refused sex, reproaching her childish behaviour when she made advances. Although publicly, despite his frailty, he maintains patriarchal authority, in private he regresses to an infantile state, demanding 'Ta' dirty! Ta' dirty!' (*OS* 155–6). Munro is exceptionally frank about the brutality and the raw hunger of sex, and her own 'rude language' has sometimes been toned down for the *New Yorker*.[3] Sexual and scatological drives are everyone's 'open secrets'. Adults collude in maintaining a distance between private behaviour and public speech, and between adolescent licence and grown-up respectability. Munro's fondness, in all her work, for images of masquerade, exposes the self-controlled, judicious adult self as a fragile construct. That fragility is often manifested through the body and in the dialogue between adult and childish forms of discourse.

Initially, Maureen 'solves' the mystery of Heather Bell's disappearance by conflating the girl's experience with her own teenage years:

> *I dare you to run away.* Was it possible? There are times when girls are inspired, when they want the risks to go on and on. They want to be heroines regardless. They want to take a joke beyond where

anybody has ever taken it before. To be careless, dauntless, to create havoc – that was the lost hope of girls. (*OS* 139)

Then there is a second 'solution', the revelation triggered by watching the couple on the wall. Maureen's glimpse into their private scenario merges with her own domestic abuse. Capturing Maureen's thought processes, Munro describes how consciousness is multi-layered; we can be thinking about several things simultaneously. In order to endure a traumatic experience, it may even be necessary to switch to another level:

> Even while it was going on she had been able to think of other things. She had thought about making a custard, she thought about whether they had enough milk and eggs. And right through her husband's rampage, she thought of the fingers moving in the feathers, the wife's hand laid on top of the husband's, pressing down. (*OS* 156)

Enid makes eggnogs, for the dying Mrs Quinn. Eggs and milk are maternal elements, and the careful preparation stands for a restoration of order and control. Maureen's intuition is compared to a vision; the hike leader, Mary Johnstone, claims to have seen Jesus. But what Maureen has glimpsed is both less substantial and more ordinary. She has seen a vague 'something' (*OS* 158) like a waking dream. In a hypnogogic state, we enter parallel realities, not so very different from the quotidian:

> She might catch herself sitting on stone steps eating cherries and watching a man coming up the steps carrying a parcel. She has never seen those steps or that man, but for an instant they seem to be part of another life that she is leading, a life just as long and complicated and strange and dull as this one. (*OS* 158)

Maureen's second 'solution' multiplies the gaps in the reader's knowledge, rather than supplying answers to the questions posed by Heather's disappearance. While making the custard, she visualizes the hand she has seen stroking the feathers pressed down on the very burner where she is stirring the pan. Marian's husband is juxtaposed with Maureen's, his powerful fingers with Lawyer Stephens's brutality. The dialogue between the two may suggest an ulterior motive in Marian's yarn about Mr Siddicup. When Maureen pictures the hand held to the stove in punishment, she sees it as its own double, 'dark as a glove or a hand's shadow' (*OS* 159). Husband and wife are literally hand in glove.

This moment at the stove constitutes another of Munro's variations on the epiphany. It is replayed endlessly in the undetermined future anticipated at the end of the story: 'In kitchens hundreds and thousands of miles away, she'll watch the soft skin form on the back of a wooden spoon and her memory will twitch, but it will not quite reveal to her this moment when she seems to be looking into an open secret, something not startling until you think of trying to tell it' (*OS* 160). The text is not unified by conventional plot resolution. Maureen's 'solutions' are unverifiable. They do not deliver the truth about Heather. But neither does the epiphany at the stove. In itself, it is inchoate; it represents that which evades articulation. When the moment recurs, Maureen also refuses full acknowledgement; her memory 'will not quite reveal'. The oxymoronic 'open secret' is the unfathomable void which threatens whatever stable, adult identity she has constructed for herself.

Whatever has happened to the real Heather, she is symbolically implicated in her disappearance. The photograph in the 'missing' poster shows her suppressing a giggle, seeming to mock those she has left behind: 'There will always be a tiny suggestion, in that, of her own free will' (*OS* 159). She remains, perpetually, the wild adolescent. Tamed by maturity, yet barred from adult autonomy, Maureen plays along with her husband's demands. No wonder she looks back to the freedom she has lost.

Tausky quotes Munro on the excitement of finding her adolescent powers as a writer, being able to 'translate a kind of rapture that ... everybody feels'. For Munro, the teenage years, before young women are fettered by marriage and motherhood, are a time of self-discovery and experimentation in general. Teenagers unleash almost magical powers, as emergent sexuality is joined with childish devilry. Female adolescence is a form of carnival, where the rules are temporarily suspended. In the *Open Secrets* collection, this theme is explored again in 'Spaceships Have Landed'. The title story of *Hateship, Friendship, Courtship, Loveship, Marriage* (2001) describes how two girls fake a series of love letters, a practical joke with unexpected results. Munro's 'rapture' is the thrill of adolescent potency. It is also the source of the 'open secret' that is writing itself, the indefinable insight that generates the artistic process – 'something not startling until you think of trying to tell it'.

The Canadian critic Linda Hutcheon claims that postmodern fiction is marked by a 'deliberate refusal to resolve contradictions'.[4] Such contradictions multiply in Munro's work, especially in the *Open Secrets* collection. Whether Heather Bell has been abducted, or has vanished in a prank that went too far, can never be established. The alternatives coexist, and may even overlap, engendering further possibilities. The ending of this story, like that of 'The Jack Randa Hotel', points to an ongoing, unfinalized reality, running far beyond the page.

When time is experienced as flux, existence resists definition. It is protean. It cannot keep still. While there are identifiable turning points and 'disarrangements' in our lives, the outcome remains unpredictable. In 'Winter Wind', the narrator says how much her mother enjoyed stories, 'particularly those full of tragedy and renunciation and queer turns of fate' (*SBM* 192). Those 'queer turns of fate' impose some kind of meaning, even though they do not supply uniformity. If events are completely random, then existence is frighteningly fragile. The high incidence of disease, disability and unnatural death in Munro's stories bears this out. But 'providence' (the title of one of the *Beggar Maid* stories) admits some kind of causal chain, albeit one which is initiated arbitrarily, and liable to sudden interventions. Carol L. Beran draws attention to Thomas Hardy's influence on Munro, especially in 'Carried Away', another story from *Open Secrets*.[5] Like Hardy, Munro shows how a concatenation of circumstance can determine a whole sequence of events. A trivial detail or a twist of fate has repercussions for characters who may be unaware of its significance. As Munro explains in her *Meanjin* interview, 'something completely unimportant really does matter'. In 'Carried Away', which I discuss in the next chapter, Louisa's future husband has no idea of her connection with the employee whose gruesome fate they discuss.

Adultery is one of the more obvious turning points in the lives of Munro's characters, though, again, it may be the product of chance, and the consequences are unpredictable. Adultery precipitates change, ending marriages which, if not exactly thrilling, did not previously seem intolerable. In 'The Children Stay' (*The Love of a Good Woman*), Pauline suddenly walks out of a family holiday to join her lover, who has followed her to Vancouver Island. She has severed all connections with her past including, it gradually dawns on her, the children, left in the holiday cottage with her husband's family. She has followed the logic of her body, forgetting other considerations; here and in other stories – for instance, 'What Is Remembered' (*Hateship, Friendship, Courtship, Loveship, Marriage*) – Munro portrays adultery as an irresistible physical impulse. Contemplating her own actions, Pauline knows that, like other adulterers, she will be regarded as 'irresponsible, immature, selfish, or even cruel. Also lucky' (*TLGW* 208). She is lucky because there are only two possible motivations. One is sex. The other is 'a faith that their shared future would be altogether different in kind from what they had in the past'.

The passage is characteristically ambiguous. Pauline's voice, an authorial voice and collective wisdom are intertwined:

> That was what Pauline must believe now – that there was this major difference in lives or in marriages or unions between people. That some of them had a necessity, a fatefulness, about them that others did not have. Of course she would have said the same thing a year ago. People did say that, they seemed to believe that, and to believe that their own cases were all of the first, the special kind, even when anybody could see that they were not and that these people did not know what they were talking about. (*TLGW* 208)

The repetition of 'people' and 'difference/different' in the story, and the conflict between the commonplace and the exceptional embodied by these terms, undermines the second alternative. A little later in the story, Pauline is unequivocal; she has given up everything for sex. The instinct which obliterates free will cannot be reduced entirely to biology; it is also, partially, a heightened state of consciousness. But it is grounded in the corporeal – 'this stripping away, the inevitable flight, the feelings she doesn't have to strive for but only to give in to like breathing or dying' (*TLGW* 210). When Pauline goes to meet her lover, she is not planning to leave her husband; the idea hits her like 'an earthquake' (*TLGW* 209), an external force beyond rational control. Losing her children is also a corporeal experience, an enduring pain 'to carry along and get used to until it's only the past she's grieving for and not any possible present' (*TLGW* 213). It is a pain which will destroy the new relationship.

Adultery is a rite of passage, but the transformation that it heralds is not as extreme as it at first appears, at least not externally. The break with the past is not absolute. Pauline does get her things back from her husband's house after all, and her daughters do not turn against her to any significant extent. But the submission to unconscious drives marks a subjective turning point, invisible to others. In 'What Is Remembered', Meriel believes, correctly, that her tryst with the flying doctor is strictly a one-off, and that her marriage will survive. However, it does open up a living daydream which she can regularly revisit without jeopardizing marital security.

Meriel's husband resembles Pauline's in his schoolboyish habits and vocabulary. Both stories balance the alternatives finely. Pauline's young, artistic lover acts impetuously; Meriel's forswears commitment. The doctor's refusal to kiss her goodbye is a warning 'to save her from the false hopes and humiliation of a certain kind of mistake' (*HFC* 241). The older Meriel ponders the adventures she might have had, if she had not heeded the warning, but she also wonders how long he kept that defensive gesture, and whether he had played another role – a role that, implicitly, she might have summoned, had she been less prudent in her own behaviour.

In a much earlier story, 'Tell Me Yes or No', it is claimed that: 'Love is not in the least unavoidable, there is a choice made. It is just that it is hard to know when the choice was made, or when, in spite of seeming frivolous, it became irreversible (*SBM* 111). In 'Dulse', Lydia is said to be typical of her generation, in that 'she has an idea of love which is ruinous but not serious in some way, not respectful' (*MJ* 54–5). 'The Children Stay' cites Anna Karenina and Madame Bovary. Meriel might also be thinking of *Anna Karenina* when she considers that in some types of story she might throw herself off the ferry after she has parted from her lover. (For readers familiar with *The Beggar Maid*, the ferry might also suggest the soap opera in 'Simon's Luck'). Both women, well versed in literary convention, toy self-consciously with these transgressive personae. Both compare romantic absolutes with real-life pragmatism. Meriel's husband, Pierre, shares his name with Tolstoy's self-effacing hero in *War and Peace*. With him, she discusses another Anna, from Turgenev's *Fathers and Sons*, an Anna who – unrealistically, she feels – spurns illicit passion.

The discussion takes place years after the adultery, when Pierre is already slowly dying. 'What Is Remembered' cuts between the marriage, the affair and Meriel's reconstruction of it. Both relationships enact a dialogue between intimacy and strangeness. Within the fantasy relationship, Meriel knows the doctor as well as her own husband, yet the intensity of her subjective experience remains hidden from both men. 'The Children Stay' also parallels the marriage and affair, novelty and familiarity. The husband and the lover seem very different from one another, yet ultimately they are interchangeable, and Pauline is no better off with one than the other.

Pauline's affair begins when she is playing Eurydice in Anouilh's version of the Orpheus myth. For her, as for Eurydice, who is first rescued from death and then lost again, there is no turning back. Like her nineteenth-century prototypes, she has risked everything for a single act of folly. Adultery, for Munro's heroines, is a means of escape, a form of flight. Their lovers often are literally airborne, like the pilot in 'White Dump' (*The Progress of Love*). They appear out of the blue, swiftly wreaking havoc in a marriage. Adultery is an accident waiting to happen.

Erotic love is another manifestation of contingency, a random event which brings irreversible change: as 'The Children Stay' puts it, 'her life was falling forwards' (*TLGW* 209). In seeming to exercise free will, Pauline finds herself imprisoned by the loss of her children. 'A fluid choice, the choice of fantasy, is poured out on the ground and instantly hardens; it has taken its undeniable shape' (*TLGW* 212).

No matter how dramatic these turning points may be, their chief interest lies in the different types of discourse they engender. In all of these stories, fantasy and reality intersect. A mysterious death or an amorous encounter is constructed and reconstructed through the many layers of memory, imagination and textuality – something 'you think of trying to tell' (*OS* 160). Munro's *Meanjin* interview raises the possibility of parallel universes. But these worlds do not simply run alongside referential reality. They cross back and forth, into one another, creating irresolvable mysteries.

6

Reconstructing the Past

'What Is Remembered' shows how selective memory can be – rewriting the past, erasing some details, while retaining or inventing others. It begins with the gloves Meriel wore at a funeral in her youth, which reminded her at the time of something she read in a magazine: 'a quote within a quote – something Queen Sirkit said that Balmain had said' (*HFC* 219). The gloves are a minor detail in a day which ought to be momentous for her husband – it's his best friend's funeral – but is less significant to Meriel, until her fling with the doctor which, in itself, appears to have little impact on her day-to-day life. It is on the way home, as it turns into memory, that the encounter gathers force:

> What she had to go through was wave after wave of intense recollection. And this was what she would continue to go through – at gradually lengthening intervals – for years to come. She would keep picking up things she'd missed, and these would still jolt her. (*HFC* 271)

Memory is a text which is re-inscribed with each new reading. Munro distrusts a tendency in art to reduce lived experience to formulaic patterns. But she also reveals ways in which memory itself aestheticizes, by editing past experience. In her memory, Meriel has substituted a fading hotel for the apartment where she had sex with the doctor.

Bergson, the philosopher who most influenced modernist fiction, argues that memory is implicit in every perception. Even as the present moment is unfolding, it is already being reconstituted:

> Your perception, however instantaneous, consists then of an incalculable multitude of remembered elements; in truth, every

71

perception is already memory. *Practically we perceive only the past,*
the pure present being the invisible progress of the past gnawing
into the future.[1]

Memories and perceptions infuse one another, and this
permutation of past and present is one of the distinctive
elements in Munro's fiction. As Meriel learns, the past
cannot be recovered intact. Memories are conditioned by
time's passing, and by the perspectives of the present.
This process is under way even before she has boarded
the ferry back home. As the years go by, her memory
elaborates on the affair, adding some details not originally
present, or which may have been temporarily forgotten.
Munro's stories often describe objects that have been abandoned and are then reclaimed – the optometrist's instruments
in 'The Love of a Good Woman' or the family home
in 'The Progress of Love' (*The Progress of Love*). Such
things bring together resurrection and decay, Bergson's
'invisible progress of the past'.

In 'The Progress of Love', the narrator revisits her old home
when it's up for sale. Since she lived there, it has changed its
character several times, most notably as a hippy commune.
There is just one corner where the wallpaper has not been
properly stripped, so that the layers added by the inhabitants
still remain. A pattern she recognizes from childhood is just
about visible. But as she tries to uncover it, the whole patch
comes away in her hands.

But the most important object still remaining is the stove
where the narrator's mother burnt three thousand dollars. She
burnt the money because it was an inheritance from the father
she had despised since childhood, and so the stove provides a
link with family lore.

The first-person narrator is never addressed by name. But
she informs us that she was christened 'Euphemia'. The family
used the less cumbersome soubriquet 'Phemie'; 'Fame', the
name she devised for herself in adult life, has not suited her
either. Her mother also had another name in childhood – her
given name, Marietta – but it has fallen into disuse. Her
husband calls her Mother. 'Marietta' is transmuted into a
character in the melodramatic tales she tells her daughter:

Marietta, in my mind, was separate, not swallowed up in my mother's grown-up body. Marietta was still running around loose up in her town of Ramsay, on the Ottawa River. In that town, the streets were full of horses and puddles, and darkened by men who came in from the bush on weekends. (PL 9)

This Marietta is the joint invention of the mother's stories and the daughter's imagination, a 'marionette'. 'Marietta' is also a diminutive form of 'Mary', the ultimate mother, the mother of God. Names are often charged with secret meanings in Munro. There is a whole cluster of 'm's in 'Open Secrets' – Maureen, Marion, Mary; Marion Hubbard's surname is also a slurred rendition of 'Heather Bell'. 'M', of course, stands for 'Mother', a word that disturbs the young narrator in 'Images' (DHS 1968):

She spoke of herself gloomily in the third person, saying, 'Be careful, don't hurt Mother, don't sit on Mother's legs.' Every time she said Mother I felt chilled, and a kind of wretchedness and shame spread through me as it did at the name of Jesus. (DHS 33)

Naming the mother breaches a taboo, forcing definition on the ineffable. It separates the maternal, threatening the dissolution of a subjectivity founded on its presence. In 'The Progress of Love', the uncertainty about the narrator's name stands for a shifting sense of identity, founded in the relationship with the mother. The focalization shifts, as the narrator identifies with the fictionalized Marietta. But the story's protagonist, in dramatic terms, is 'Marietta's mother', another unnamed character – although we can guess her name if we remember that the narrator was named after her. This Euphemia's role is that of the persecuted heroine, driven to the edge by a callous husband. The 'Marietta' version of her attempted suicide is contradicted by the narrator's Aunt Beryl, on a whirlwind visit that recalls Uncle Bill's appearance in Lives of Girls and Women. She reads Euphemia's preparations to hang herself as a put-on, meant to punish her husband for stepping out of line – a prank which, admittedly, went a little too far.

In 'The Progress of Love', identity is multi-faceted. It is delineated through family relationships, and particularly through the 'reading' of memories. Images of the narrator's girlhood are overlaid by her mother's stories, which are themselves re-assembled through Phemie's – and through Fame's – fantasy. The three generations of women exchange names and subject positions. Those who would like to pursue the Bakhtinian approach introduced in chapter 4 will find this account of selfhood as mutual exchange echoed in his writing. Bakhtin claims that the self is also constructed through an infinite dialogue: 'As we gaze at each other, two different worlds are reflected in the pupils of our eyes.'[2]

Fame – if this is what we should call the adult narrator – has a story she tells, about her father watching her mother slowly burn the money. She knows that this is not factually correct. Her mother told Beryl she burnt the money, but she carried out the act in secret. Nevertheless, the image of her father standing by, without interfering, is as tangible as anything that 'really' happened. It is rendered more fully than her marriage to Dan Casey, a man who is named, but about whom we are told next to nothing.

Munro's characters try to sort their lives, and those of others, into a plausible narrative form. But ongoing experience escapes neat definitions, and efforts to retrieve past memories are constantly defeated by the inevitable gaps and inconsistencies. In the old house, the narrator lets her boyfriend believe that she is in a bad mood because the room with the wallpaper was her room as a child; the lie simplifies her emotions and conforms to narrative expectations. But she is disturbed by her own mythmaking, and by her mother's, which blocks off further questions by imposing closure:

> Her heart was broken. That was what I always heard my mother say. That was the end of it. Those words lifted up the story and sealed it shut. (*PL* 13)

In fiction, a broken heart kills, and the concept of a story 'sealed ... shut' implies the sealing of a coffin. The story is closed, but it is also constantly reiterated, its key phrases echoing in the narrator's consciousness:

> Marietta's mother laughed after not hanging herself. She sat at Mrs. Sutcliffe's table long ago and laughed. Her heart was broken. (*PL* 13)

This is carnival laughter, ambivalent laughter which leaves the Marietta story unresolved.

Each person's version of an essential self – the 'real me' – may be only a fiction, but it is necessary in our everyday lives. In order to function as autonomous beings, we need to ignore the extent to which we have been 'authored' in a relationship with real and imaginary others. For some women, as we saw in chapter 2, this sense of personal autonomy may be threatened by an over-identification with the mother. In 'The Progress of Love', the mother is a highly ambivalent figure, stoking an imaginative and emotional hunger in the daughter that can never be satisfied. The narrator observes that her mother's words work their power only on herself, not on her brothers: 'And when I just had the two boys myself, no daughters, I felt as if something could stop now – the stories and griefs, the old puzzles you can't resist or solve' (PL 14).

'There was a cloud, a poison, that had touched my mother's life' (PL 13). This image of the cloud, something all-pervasive, yet formless, can be read in relation to the mother's pronouncements on hatred: 'One drop of hatred in your soul will spread and discolor everything like a drop of black ink in white milk' (PL 6). The mother's words are deeply ironic in the context of her own, carefully nurtured hatred towards her own father. But it is the ink, spreading another kind of cloud within the maternal element that is especially interesting. Once again, Munro uses the word 'shame' and links maternal authority with the divine. When she has displeased her mother, the narrator feels that she is part of the poisonous cloud. When she tries to atone, she is told to ask God for forgiveness:

> But it wasn't God, it was my mother I had to get straight with. It seemed as if she knew something about me that was worse, far worse, than ordinary lies and tricks and meanness; it was a really sickening shame. (PL 13)

The passage shows the daughter's difficulty in differentiating herself from the mother. Like God, she is omniscient; lacking privacy, the daughter lacks control. Burdened by this sense of indefinable 'shame', she feels responsible for her mother's depressive moods. 'Shame', as ever, doubles on itself, running back and forth between the two of them.

'The Progress of Love' is one of several stories where a first-person narrator reassesses family history. Comparing contradictory interpretations of the past, she realizes that they have been mediated not only in the telling but in their reception. They have been conditioned by her own subjectivity, including a tendency to fit lived experience into a unified narrative, as if it were fiction. This is particularly evident in the 'Chaddeleys and Flemings' sequence in *The Moons of Jupiter* (1982). Family history is endlessly recounted, and embodied in a network of visiting relations. In 'Family Furnishings' (*Hateship, Friendship, Courtship, Loveship, Marriage*, 2001), a very ordinary childhood anecdote acquires a deeper significance when it is retold by a newly discovered family member. Cousin Alfrida's secret love-child disputes common knowledge, and betrays disturbing insights into the narrator's personality. In stories like these, the past runs into the present. Family history forms a continuum with the narrator's autobiography. The narrator investigates her own past through writing, in a process that always pushes ahead, resisting symbolic resolution:

> If I had been making a proper story out of this, I would have ended it, I think, with my mother not answering and going ahead of me across the pasture. That would have done. I didn't stop there, I suppose, because I wanted to find out more, remember more. ('The Ottawa Valley', *SBM* 234–5)

In 'The Ottawa Valley' and in two other stories in *Something I've Been Meaning to Tell You*, 'Material' and 'Winter Wind', Munro refers to the 'tricks' at the writer's disposal. In 'The Ottawa Valley', 'the only problem is my mother':

> She is as heavy as always, she weighs everything down, and yet she is indistinct, her edges melt and flow. Which means she has stuck to me as close as ever and refused to fall away, and I could go on and on, applying what skills I have, using what tricks I know, and it would always be the same. (*SBM* 235)

'Trick' is used slightly differently, as a verb, in 'Winter Wind'. The narrator accuses herself of having 'tricked . . . out' real people, remodelling them to suit her artistic purpose. In

'Material', the narrator compares her own memories of a neighbour with the fictional version published by her ex-husband: 'There is Dotty lifted out of life and held in light, suspended in the marvellous clear jelly that Hugo has spent all his life learning how to make' (*SBM* 48). The ceaseless flow of duration has been arrested. Lived experience, which is protean and boundless, has been petrified into art.

'Tricks' imply fraudulence. Yet they also work magic. Munro's ambivalence towards artistry is expressed in an essay published just before *Something I've Been Meaning to Tell You*:

> Even as I most feverishly, desperately practise it, I am a little afraid that the work with words may turn out to be a questionable trick, an evasion (and never more so than when it is most dazzling, apt and striking), an unavoidable lie.[3]

In both 'Material' and 'The Ottawa Valley', the narrators grudgingly admire these 'lovely tricks, honest tricks' (*SBM* 48). Interviewed by Graeme Gibson, Munro suggests that writers find compensation for a lack of control over their own lives by ordering fictional experience.[4]

Autobiographical forms of discourse heighten the sense of time as flux, since an autobiography, written by the living subject, must, by definition, be unfinished. The stories are elaborated by retelling and by fresh information, but never reach completion. Munro's incorporation of these forms of discourse should not be taken as a guarantee of referential truth. While she sees personal experience as a powerhouse for her work, she is also careful to disavow any specific correspondences between its content and her own life, sometimes prefacing collections with a disclaimer. In an introduction available in some editions of *The Moons of Jupiter*, she says that 'Some of these stories are closer to my own life than others are, but not one of them is as close as people seem to think' (*MJ* xiii). She discusses how a textual logic, independent of the original impulse behind a story, develops during the writing. Authorial intention succumbs to unconscious influences, and external observation merges with interiority:

> The stories that are personal are carried inexorably away from the real. And the observed stories lose their anecdotal edges, being invaded by familiar shapes and voices. (*MJ* xiv)

Autobiography is one of the range of discursive strategies Munro brings to each story. Sometimes she invites the reader to compare life and fiction, for instance in the references to Tolstoy and Turgenev in 'What Is Remembered' and 'The Children Stay'. 'The Children Stay' is also a rereading of Anouilh's version of the Orpheus myth (another 'quote within a quote'). The experience of reading is intertwined with reality, conditioning all other aspects.

Like the American writers she admires – Eudora Welty, Katherine Ann Porter, Willa Cather – Munro sees small-town life as the locus of change and continuity. Widespread historical developments – world wars, mass education, female emancipation – are enacted in microcosm. In a small, enclosed community, she can explore the close connections between families and individuals, and, most importantly, what they know about each other:

> Even in that close-mouthed place, stories were being made. People carried their stories around with them. My grandmother carried hers, and nobody ever spoke of it to her face. ('Winter Wind', *SBM* 193)

Munro explores the fictional towns which recur in her work – Walley, Jubilee, Carstairs, Hanratty – through strategies associated with local and oral history. Recording your own history is especially important in a postcolonial country like Canada, which is marking out its identity – or rather, identities, reflecting the diversity of immigrant and pioneer cultures. In contrast to the grand narrative sweep of old-fashioned imperial history, local and popular history, the history of families and communities, entails a piecing together of fragmentary evidence. It is often the preserve of enthusiastic amateurs who may be found, as Munro describes them in 'Menesteung', 'going around with notebooks, scraping dirt off gravestones, reading microfilm, just in the hope of seeing this trickle in time, making a connection, rescuing one thing from the rubbish' (*FMY* 73).

Schoolroom history places well-documented events, like the Edict of Nantes 'The Love of a Good Woman' or the Peace of Utrecht (*Dance of the Happy Shades*), in logical succession, identifying clear causes and effects. The local historian deals with material which is ever-present, yet also insubstantial. The past is disappearing fast, but it is still made tangible in the fabric of a house, in local streets and buildings. If anything, there is a surfeit of evidence. In 'Heirs of the Living Body' (*Lives of Girls and Women*, 1971), Uncle Craig is compiling a history of the county. He is so scrupulous about including every detail that by the time of his death he has only got as far as 1909. Oral storytelling also brings the past to life, but, as in 'The Progress of Love', it cannot be relied upon to produce a single, authenticated view.

Bakhtin borrows the term 'chronotope' from relativist science to specify the artistic configuration of the space–time nexus. Time's forward progression in the historical novel, as practised by Tolstoy or Stendhal, may be contrasted with cyclical time in novels of provincial life, such as Flaubert's *Madame Bovary*. In the provincial town, time seems to stand still. 'Time here has no advancing historical movement; it moves rather in narrow circles: the circle of the day, of the week, of the month, of a person's entire life.'[5] Since, by definition, nothing happens, major events cannot take place within this chronotope, but it provides a background against which they unfold. The communities Munro describes are often touched by change; farmhouses are converted into rural retreats or hippy communes. But they also represent continuity, and are embedded within this 'provincial' chronotope. In *The Beggar Maid*, Rose returns to Hanratty to find her old schoolmates still there, in different circumstances, but basically unchanged. Provincial life remains static, but it also stands for universality. The everyday is re-enacted across time and continents, from Chekhov's Russia to Mansfield's New Zealand and Cather's Midwest. When, speaking about Munro, Lorrie Moore says, 'Although she writes of the provinces she is the least provincial writer I know', the paradox is not entirely inexplicable.[6]

Munro often uses letters as evidence, when she incorporates historical forms of discourse. Letters are a vital source, combining the immediacy of direct discourse with the permanence of writing. They collapse time and space, speaking directly from the past. But they are also dated precisely, situating events at an irrecoverable distance: 'Miss Margaret

Cresswell, Matron, House of Industry, Toronto, to Mr. Simon Herron, North Huron, January 15, 1852' (*OS* 190). Letter-writing is a vital part of the colonial and postcolonial experience. The correspondence between settlers and homeland crosses the divide between them, and, in describing the new world, colonists build a new reality for the benefit of those they have left behind. The *Open Secrets* collection draws extensively on letters to explore different kinds of migration. 'A Wilderness Station' uses epistolary form almost entirely, juxtaposing contradictory versions of events in the 1850s. 'Carried Away' interweaves many different speech genres, bringing together elements from romantic and historical fiction, local history and tales of the supernatural. It is also a tale of provincial life. Events are enacted against the chronotopic background which Bakhtin associates with stasis.

Traditionally, letter-writing has been especially important to women. Like 'How I Met My Husband' and 'Tell Me Yes or No' (*Something I've Been Meaning to Tell You*), 'Carried Away' highlights the emotional charge invested in letters received, written or waited for by women who are in love. Love letters transport the reader out of clock time, suspending the quotidian; the title story in *Hateship, Friendship, Courtship, Loveship, Marriage* shows their power to transform lives through romance. Like Meriel's fantasies in 'What Is Remembered', love letters are at least as exciting as actual experience, and perhaps even more so, since they are predicated on anticipation, rather than satisfaction. They demonstrate the power of discourse to construct a subjective reality.

'Carried Away' opens early in 1917, with an exchange of letters between Louisa, the Carstairs librarian, and Jack Agnew, a wounded soldier. According to his first letter, Jack is writing as a distraction in hospital, and because he is intrigued by the educated stranger who has reorganized the library. Louisa's motive in replying, six weeks later, may be to replace the illicit correspondence with a married lover which has left such a gap in her life that it has driven her out of the city into the provinces. Jack's next missive, sent from the western front, mixes clumsy colloquial language with a heightened literary style, evoking specific moments through imagery:

One day when I got to the Library it was a Saturday afternoon and you had just unlocked the door and were putting the lights on as it was dark and raining out. You had been caught out with no hat or umbrella and your hair had got wet. You took the pins out of it and let it come down. Is it too personal a thing to ask if you have it long still or have you cut it? You went over and stood by the radiator and shook your hair on it and the water sizzled like grease in the frying pan. (OS 7)

The incongruous metaphor contributes to the letter's naïve charm, suggesting a spontaneous sincerity. When Jack, requesting a photograph, enquires if she is engaged, the emotional temperature is raised. Although she does not remember him, Jack provides a focus for Louisa's life; in her own mind, she is now included in the fellowship of women who have something at stake in the war.

Personal letters, like this correspondence and the unsent letter at the start of 'Vandals' (OS 261–4) introduce a first-person narrative into a story told mostly through free indirect discourse. It offers the reader direct access into a character's consciousness. For the reader, as for Louisa, all we know about Jack's state of mind is revealed through the letters. While much of the story is focalized through her consciousness, Jack's subjectivity is withheld. When the war ends, Louisa waits for his return, only to read in the newspaper that he has married someone else. Within a few years, he is decapitated in an industrial accident. Unlike Louisa, whose conversations are reported from the viewpoint of two other lovers – Jim Frarey, the travelling salesman, and Arthur Doud, whom she marries – Jack is never granted direct speech. His correspondence with Louisa is recapitulated through her reported speech (she tells Jim all about him, but not Arthur); his death told several times, in the newspaper, and from Arthur's perspective.

Louisa does not ask for a photograph; later on, it bothers her that she never knew what he looked like. While Louisa's changing appearance is described several times, he remains invisible to the reader also. Arthur's family owns the piano factory, where the accident happens. Overcoming his squeamishness, he is obliged to retrieve Arthur's head:

He picked it up. He carried it delicately and securely as you might carry an awkward but valuable jug. Pressing the head out of sight, as if comforting it, against his chest. (OS 34)

81

Disembodied, Jack has become an object, devoid of subjectivity. When Louisa enquires what he looked like, Arthur tells her 'it was all – all pretty much obliterated, by that time' (OS 38).

For Jack and Louisa, the letters provide a transcendent space, removing Jack from war and Louisa from small-town existence. For Louisa, romance crosses into reality, transforming everyday existence. Jack is able to separate these spheres. He is more of a spectator than a participant in the scenes he visualizes. Even when he is implicated in them, the spotlight remains on Louisa, with the library as backdrop. Jack's least intimate letter is the one he delivers personally – one line on a scrap of paper, stuffed under a blotter: 'I was engaged before I went overseas' (OS 18). He has been back to the library, close to Louisa, but unrecognized.

Louisa's letters are more businesslike than Jack's, answering his queries with detachment. But her inner life, nurtured by reading, maintains an intensity at odds with her outward persona. Louisa 'authors' herself, constructing a subjectivity from the perspective of an imagined other. After an earlier love affair, she consoled herself with the self-image of 'a heroine of love's tragedy' (OS 9) – perhaps someone from her favourite authors, Thomas Hardy or Willa Cather. In the photograph she has taken for Jack, she would like to pose in peasant costume, something she has seen in pictures, but has to be content with her workaday self, whose expression is 'sterner and more foreboding than she had intended' (OS 10). The discourses of romantic fiction and of common-sense reality are in conflict:

> She would have said love was all hocus-pocus, a deception, and she believed that. But at the prospect she still felt a hush, a flutter along the nerves, a bowing down of sense, a flagrant prostration. (OS 10)

Munro's interest in destabilizing notions of absolute time and a single reality in the *Open Secrets* collection is especially evident in 'Carried Away'. Clock time and 'real time', or duration, are in conflict with one another, just as Louisa is divided between an intellectual and intuitive response. Like Gerald, in D. H. Lawrence's *Women in Love*, Arthur aims to be a force for rationalism, introducing modern industrial principles to the family business. Time is strictly regulated at the Doud piano factory:

> The factory whistle dictated the time for many to get up, blowing at six o'clock in the morning. It blew again for work to start at seven and at twelve for dinnertime and at one in the afternoon for work to recommence, and then at five-thirty for men to lay down their tools and go home. (*OS* 25)

The first rule, posted next to the time clock, is 'ONE MINUTE LATE IS FIFTEEN MINUTES PAY' (*OS* 25). Louisa also brings an up-to-the-minute efficiency to the library – although Arthur, as it turns out, has bypassed the system by smuggling his books out unstamped. His sudden, unpredictable death also undermines the rationalist drive towards hegemony by foregrounding human fragility and the perverse.

Munro depicts social conditions meticulously, outlining changes in working practices and the struggle to keep the factory going through the Depression and another war. But social realism is constantly disrupted, and clock time gives way to duration. Shortly after the conversation about the dead man's appearance, Arthur decides to depart from his routine for that night, which includes his monthly visit to his mistress. Here, as elsewhere in the story, Munro recreates the atmosphere of a bygone era:

> When Arthur had last paid attention to the street, he had seen plenty of daylight left; country people shopping, boys squirting each other at the drinking fountain, and young girls walking up and down in their soft, cheap, flowery summer dresses, letting the young men watch them from wherever the young men congregated – the Post Office steps, the front of the feed store. (*OS* 39)

The nostalgic detail is almost Capraesque. But when a storm disperses this tableau of small-town life, time becomes increasingly indeterminate. Inside the library, the noise of falling rain interrupts conversation. As Arthur watches Louisa, 'the Librarian', silently, in the half-light, his rationalism fails him:

> He could no more define the feeling he got from her than you can describe a smell. It's like the scorch of electricity. It's like burnt kernels of wheat. No, it's like a bitter orange. I give up. (*OS* 40)

He is experiencing 'real time', which cannot be classified or measured.

Like 'The Love of a Good Woman' (*The Love of a Good Woman*), 'Carried Away' is a novella at the start of a collection, and is subdivided into 'chapters'. The final section, 'Tolpuddle Martyrs', leaps more than thirty years ahead from the storm. Louisa has married Arthur, and been widowed. On a trip to see a heart specialist in London, Ontario, she is hot and tired, and becomes disoriented. A Jack Agnew is advertised as a trade union speaker at the laying of a memorial. He greets her; they catch up on one another's lives; this is her Jack, the man who wrote the letters. But this Jack was not killed at the factory shortly after the First World War.

Entering this alternative universe, Louisa has 'gone under a wave' (*OS* 50):

> It was anarchy she was up against – a devouring muddle. Sudden holes and impromptu tricks and radiant vanishing consolations. (*OS* 50)

The wave metaphor foreshadows the orgasmic 'wave after wave of intense recollection' in 'What Is Remembered'. Although the symptoms are unnerving, they are also gratifying. Before her marriage, Louisa was partial to a glass of wine. She is undergoing something like inebriation in her current condition.

While 'The Progress of Love' implies that lived experience is conditioned by textuality, Munro's recent work emphasizes narrative pleasure. Like drink, drugs or sex, storytelling induces an altered state, grounded in the body. The escape from clock time is expressed through heightened physical sensations. Munro is too sceptical a writer to propose that these liminal states reveal a single, unchanging reality such as that posited by Bergson. Rather, she suggests that we construct multiple selves, switching, in fantasy and in reality, between parallel lives.

'Sudden holes and impromptu tricks' recalls the 'deep holes, ominous beckoning places' that Munro imagined in the river where she played (EH). As Robert Thacker points out, a river represents the passage of time.[7] The sudden drop down the hole removes us from that onward flow, diverting us into all kinds of random possibilities. 'Carried Away' is full of openings into other dimensions, whether they are intertextual echoes, references to other Munro stories or dialogic interplay within the text itself.

Linearity is further suspended through time shifts and multiple viewpoints. This fragmentation begins with the letters, and the movement between first and third-person narration. In the remaining three-quarters of the text, the viewpoint drifts not only between Louisa, Jim Frarey and Arthur, but also between Louisa just after the war and her older self in the fifties.

The story ends with a beginning. In its closing sequence, it returns to wartime, and Louisa's sudden impulse to take over at the library. Once again, Munro evokes a bygone age, through concise period detail; we know Carstairs's population and the layout of the streets. The mood in the final paragraph is almost nostalgic:

> As evening came on, big blinkered horses with feathered hooves pulled the sleighs across the bridge, past the hotel, beyond the street lights, down the dark side roads. Somewhere out in the country they would lose the sound of each other's bells. (*OS* 51)

The snowy scene recalls the close of Joyce's 'The Dead'. Like Joyce, Munro uses images of landscape, weather and approaching darkness to evoke transience. Attention is turned away from the handful of characters in the story, towards the universal. The 'feathered hooves' suggest the speed at which time passes, marking the insignificance of our short lives.

Appropriating historical types of discourse, Munro shows how close they are to fiction. Even so, the historian must look for coherent explanations, aiming at what is probable, rather than possible. Fiction-making is an extension of daydreams and of childish make-believe. In fiction, we can inhabit several worlds at once. Nothing defeats mortality, but fiction can suspend time for a while.

7

Ageing, Decay, Abjection

Although we experience time as a seamless continuum, our bodies remind us that it also moves irreversibly forwards. We are all getting older every day. Mortality, sickness and decay have pervaded Munro's fiction from the start, often carnivalized, through grotesque imagery. As she enters her seventies, her characters' lives are increasingly overshadowed by illness and bereavement. Time is running out for many of the couples in *Hateship, Friendship, Courtship, Loveship, Marriage*. Their relationships have been less than perfect, but the severance forced, inevitably, by mortality unbalances their day-to-day existence. In 'Floating Bridge', Jinny is a mere 42, her husband sixteen years older. Suffering from cancer, she is obliged to reconsider her assumptions about their long-term future. In 'Comfort', Nina tries to follow the wishes of her proudly Darwinian husband, by dispensing with the customary funeral rites. The final story, 'The Bear Came Over the Mountain', describes the impact of Alzheimer's on a couple whose shared history seems to vanish as the wife's memory gradually disintegrates. But, like Parkinson's disease in Munro's earlier stories, its progress is partial, and Fiona's previous personality still resurfaces occasionally. Something of ourselves endures through time.

The characters in these latest stories welcome such small mercies. They know they have to make the most of whatever time is left. 'Floating Bridge' closes with 'a swish of tender hilarity, getting the better of all her sores and hollows, for the time given' (*HFC* 85). At the end of 'Comfort', Nina finally scatters her husband's ashes by the roadside:

Doing this was like wading and then throwing yourself into the lake for the first icy swim in June – a sickening shock at first, then amazement that you were still moving, lifted up on a stream of steely devotion – calm above the surface of your life, surviving, though the pain of the cold continued to wash into your body. (HFC 155)

When Munro was a young mother, she struggled to find time to write everything down. Now there is a fear of winding down, 'as if, if I stopped, I could be stopped for good' (PR 261). This is 'the beast that's lurking in the closet in old age' (PR 262), the dread of losing energy and purpose. By confronting such fears, the stories exorcise them. Unfolding within an ever-changing present, they find consolation in the fast-approaching, but unpredictable future.

With each Munro collection, separate narratives are in dialogue, both inside individual stories and between them. If we look more widely, across the whole body of writing, we can trace an entire network of cultural, literary and biographical interconnections. Munro constantly revisits her invented communities in Jubilee and Walley. But she scarcely needs to give a name to her imagined landscape of small towns, rivers, lakes and isolated farmsteads. Munro's territory has become familiar to her regular readers. It is a real place, southwestern Ontario, closely observed, with attention to detail. It also shades into a more mysterious, private geography, full of dark corners, deep waters and places to hide. Many who have not even visited Canada will nonetheless feel at home in this mythological landscape. When we read 'Images' (DHS) or 'The Love of a Good Woman', the axeman in the bushes and the car submerged in the pond are relocated to the places we remember from our own childhood. For Munro's adult characters, landscape retains its transformational qualities. 'Floating Bridge' provides one of the best examples of Munro's use of landscape to suggest indeterminacy. In the darkness, a stranger takes Jinny for a ride through the woods, crossing 'Borneo Swamp'. Suddenly the road turns into wooden planks. Standing on them, she feels as if she's on a boat:

And the water seemed so still, but it could not really be still because if you tried to keep your eye on one reflected star, you saw

> how it winked and changed shape and slid from sight. Then it was
> back again – but maybe not the same one. (*HFC* 84)

Metamorphosis is all around, in the natural world and in our own lives. Munro's fiction embraces the uncertainties of change, for good or ill. The stories are open structures, comparable to the mythic cycles of oral tradition. Like the Homeric storyteller, who is never committed to print, Munro retells her material within each story, recasting key elements and altering perspectives. She also reviews material between different stories, most obviously the figure of the mother, a character some readers will interpret in the context of earlier versions. By mingling autobiographical, literary and historical conventions, she blurs the distinctions between art and life.

In other words, the whole body of work may be viewed organically, and like an organism it is constantly changing and growing. A story may not only be received differently, according to whether it is read in the *New Yorker* or in sequence within a collection; it may also have changed between magazine publication and book form. The version of 'Queenie' included in *Hateship, Friendship, Courtship, Loveship, Marriage* is slightly different to the version published by Profile Books, which originally appeared in the *London Review of Books* on 30 July 1998. An explanatory last sentence, added in the proofs of the collection, has been removed before final publication.

In this concluding chapter, I am returning, once again, to *Open Secrets*, the collection most explicitly concerned with ideas about time. While in some respects it is her most diverse collection, the stories are also subtly interconnected, particularly those set in Walley and Carstairs. Unlike *Lives of Girls and Women* and *The Beggar Maid*, *Open Secrets* does not follow a strictly chronological sequence. But the stories are arranged to suggest the passing of time. Bea Doud, who is a major character in the final story, 'Vandals', has made two fleeting appearances already – as Arthur's daughter in the first story, 'Carried Away', and as Billy's alcoholic sister in the penultimate piece, 'Spaceships Have Landed'. Time leaves its mark both on Bea and on the town of Carstairs, where most of the stories are set. 'Vandals' closes the book on a valedictory note, its more contemporary setting resonating against the historical material in 'Carried Away'. Both stories close on images of snow – the image which also begins 'My Mother's Dream', the final story in *The Love of a Good Woman*.

In 'Vandals', Bea Doud's house in the country, empty since her partner, Ladner, died, has been, apparently, broken into and trashed. Unknown to her, the people responsible for the damage are the young Christian couple, Liza and Warren, who were sent to check on the place. As usual, the story is structured around a complex network of analepses, subverting linear causality. The timescale is indeterminate; we do not know, for instance, how long Bea lived with Ladner. Narrative turning points, such as Liza's religious conversion, are frequently elided, and the viewpoint is divided not just between the characters but also between their younger and older selves. These shifting viewpoints create conflicts in the reader's identification with the characters, as we learn about Liza's responsibility for wrecking the house and the motive for her actions.

The story opens with a favourite Munro device, the letter. As in previous examples, a character's inner speech is hybridized with a familiar speech genre, creating a tension between interiority and generic conformity. Bea parodies Liza's Christianity, transposing biblical language into the conventions of a thank you letter:

> 'Liza, my dear, I have never written you yet to thank you for going out to our house (poor old Dismal, I guess it really deserves the name now) in the teeth or anyway the aftermath of the storm last February and for letting me know what you found there. Thank your husband, too, for taking you out on his snowmobile, also, if as I suspect he was the one to board up the broken window to keep out the savage beasts, etc. Lay not up treasure on earth where moth and dust not to mention teenagers doth corrupt.' (*OS* 261)

We have already used Bakhtinian ideas about dialogue and the grotesque to analyse Munro's parodic language. I am now going to introduce some psychoanalytical concepts used by Julia Kristeva. Kristeva posits two interrelated tendencies in language. The 'semiotic' has its origins in the maternal body which, in an early, prelinguistic state, we do not differentiate from our own, or from the world at large. Our earliest existence is experienced as free-flowing rhythms, sounds and impulse. Anything which reminds us of the physicality of speech is a manifestation of the semiotic – its sensual qualities, rhythmic and sound patterns, even obscenities and puns. With the emergence of a distinctive self-image, separated from our environment, the second, 'symbolic' modality comes into play. The symbolic regulates the semiotic, introducing logic and meaning. Language needs the symbolic, in order to make sense; but in a literary text the semiotic charge undermines fixed meanings.

The multiple meanings at play in Munro's story are produced largely through this semiotic charge. Bea's broken syntax seems natural in an impromptu letter, but it also contributes to the disruption of stylistic unity, along with the biblical parody and the intertextual use of letters in itself. As we have come to expect in a Munro story, there are numerous other intertextual devices, including children's rhymes and the quotations from Rousseau and Aristotle which Ladner fastens to his trees. Munro uses sound patterns in names: 'Bea. Bzz. My name is Bea' (*OS* 284). The onomatopoeic 'z' links the two women's names, as well as adding to the story's animal imagery. (Ladner stuffs animals and birds, arranging them in tableaux across his land.) Nonsense words exploit the material properties of language; 'Liza Minnelli, stick it in your belly!' the adult Liza murmurs as, re-entering Bea and Ladner's house, she regresses to childhood (*OS* 283).

The patterning of names is also evident in the long initial letter. Liza's name initiates an invocatory rhythm in the story's first two paragraphs. But it is the homophonous 'Ladner', at the start of the third, who dominates the rest of Bea's letter – a letter which is unsent, and for the most part unwritten. In a sense, the letter is addressed to this man, whose silence early in their relationship prefigures that of the grave:

> *One night I got into his bed and he did not take his eyes from his book or move or speak a word to me even when I crawled out and returned to my own bed, where I fell asleep almost at once because I think I could not bear the shame of being awake.*
>
> *In the morning he got into my bed and all went as usual.*
> *I come up against blocks of solid darkness.*   (*OS* 274)

The italics indicate another of the 'letters' Bea is writing in her head. The letters give direct access to Bea's consciousness, while Ladner's inner life remains a secret. The women are assigned a diffuse and complex subjectivity which is withheld from the male characters. Although some of the story is focalized through Warren, he remains essentially a passive witness.

The long initial letter is eventually taken over by a complicated dream. In this dream, the deceased Ladner's bones are conflated with those of a 'little girl' (OS 263). Bea supposes that she is confusing this child with Liza's dead brother, Kenny. However, the pattern of names suggests a displacement from Ladner to Liza, and a repressed bond between the two.

Like many Munro women, Bea finds a transcendent pleasure in sexual encounters, allied to, but distinct from, physical consummation: 'She felt the first signal of a love affair like warmth of the sun on her skin, like music through a doorway, or the instant, as she had often said, when the black-and-white television bursts into color' (OS 265). The sensuous combination of texture, light and fleeting sound recalls Kristeva's account of infant consciousness – 'the breast, given and withdrawn; lamplight capturing the gaze; intermittent sounds of voice or music'.[1] It is in the 'nature' of women like Bea to seek out 'an insanity which could contain them' (OS 268), almost like a womb.

What matters is the intensity of the obsession. In this respect, Ladner's particular interests are irrelevant, his 'insanity' irreducible to a specific pursuit. He could be a fisherman or a football fanatic. Kristeva and other French theorists have a term for the utmost pleasure – 'jouissance', a sensation so extreme that we lose ourselves, and time seems to be suspended. We are as one, again, with the maternal body. Bea does not appear to be as literary as Louisa in 'Carried Away', but, judging by the evidence in 'Spaceships Have Landed', she is a drinker. The altered states induced by love, drink and fiction are intertwined in this collection, and all are species of jouissance.

So, to an extent, Ladner stands for the maternal. But he also represents paternal law, associated with the 'symbolic' drive towards order and control. He regulates nature, laying paths and boundaries, and writing labels with 'tight, accurate, complicated information' (OS 271). His library consists of

complete sets of histories. He does not waste words. He is
known only by his surname, an option not usually available to
women. Most importantly, he is a taxidermist. Taxidermy
operates as a kind of code; the preserved corpse is a sign
standing for the living animal, which is gone forever.
Psychoanalytic theory argues that all signification is founded
on absence and loss. We start naming things when they
become separate from ourselves – when we are cut off from
that all-embracing maternal universe we experience in infancy.

Ladner shifts between the semiotic and the symbolic –
between the maternal and the paternal absence. He names and
orders, laying down paternal law, yet he rejects rationalist,
institutionalized learning when he reacts angrily to the idea of
a school visit. On his first walk with Bea, he hurries her past
the quotations on the trees, as if conscious of their limitations.
She loses her sense of direction and the boundaries of his
property seem to dissolve. She is re-entering maternal territory.

Another concept taken from Kristeva, that of abjection,
might help clarify these ambiguities. The 'abject' is represented
by those substances that are neither self nor other. Bodily
fluids and human waste are part of ourselves, yet pass beyond
us. Saliva, tears, faeces and blood must be expelled in order to
establish a clean, autonomous self, divisible from the world
around it. Cultural taboos, such as those surrounding menstru-
ation, and private taboos, such as phobias, are expressions of
abjection. But the 'abject' can never be fully expunged. Thus,
abjection stands on the border between self and other, inside
and outside, life and death. It is grounded in the subject's need
to detach itself from the maternal; it is the mother who first
regulates the infant body, and the maternal itself must be
abjected in order to forge an independent subjectivity. We are
simultaneously repelled by the abject and compelled towards
it. Abjection is 'a deep well of memory that is unapproachable
and intimate'.[2] It is a source of enormous cathartic energy,
which may be tapped at the risk of losing your hold on
identity. In her book *Powers of Horror*, Kristeva identifies the
subversive potential of the abject in literature.

In 'Vandals', both Bea and Liza enact purification rituals,
although in Liza's case this is also an act of defilement. Bea
dreams that she is collecting Ladner's bones 'just as if I were

getting my annual load of salvia or impatiens' (*OS* 362). The association with summer bedding plants, the green aprons and the green plastic bags in which the bones are kept all suggest regeneration. Ladner's bones have been stored for seven years after his death. Seven is a mystical number in biblical and other ancient traditions. Levitical purifications lasted seven days. Nevertheless, Bea is uncertain if this is a pagan or a Christian ceremony. When she asks other people in the dream, she realizes that her question breaks a social taboo, confirming her status as an outsider: 'I've lived around here all my life, but still I get this look' (*OS* 263). The Christian/pagan antinomy, implicit in the title, is one of several sets of apparent oppositions in 'Vandals' – notably outside/inside, animal/human. The boundaries between each category give way during the course of the story. It is the Christians, Liza and Warren, who vandalize Ladner's house. When the humans have finished the damage they have wreaked from the inside, Warren boards up the windows so that animals are unable to gain access from the outside.

After her conversion to Christianity, Liza imposes strict rules on herself, abstaining from sugar and alcohol and maintaining a regimented lifestyle: 'She did the laundry every Wednesday night and counted the strokes when she brushed her teeth and got up early in the morning to do knee bends and read Bible verses' (*OS* 276). Liza has to be especially scrupulous because, unlike Warren, she is sometimes possessed by a 'crazy, slithery spirit' (*OS* 280). If you are going to be a saint, you need to be seriously tempted.

The impulses she has suppressed reassert themselves, as Liza lays waste Ladner's house. Food loathing is one of the most basic forms of abjection; by refusing food, the child insists on separation from the mother. Like an infant in its high chair, Liza throws food around, turning it to waste matter. She is reducing Ladner's house to refuse. Order is overturned. The boundaries between contrasting elements, and between the organic and inorganic are shattered: 'Liza stepped delicately among the torn, spattered books and broken glass, the smeared, stomped birds, the pools of whisky and maple syrup and the sticks of charred wood dragged from the stove to make black tracks on the rugs, the ashes and gummed flour and feathers' (*OS* 282). Treading carefully, Liza asserts her immunity to this desecration.

Foodstuff is also transformed into blood, in an unconscious mockery of the Eucharist: crème de menthe becomes 'dark-green blood' (*OS* 281), and Warren tries to repeat his teenage trick of writing in ketchup for blood – blood which belongs both to the writer and to the intended victim. Liza writes '*The Wages of Sin is Death*' in magic marker on the kitchen wall (*OS* 283), parodying her own Christian beliefs and mocking patriarchal law.

Amongst all these transgressive acts, the damage done to Ladner's stuffed birds is probably the most significant. In any circumstances, stuffed animals are unnerving creatures, things which at first appear animate, but are actually corpses. Norman Bates's stuffed birds provide the first hint of abnormality in Hitchcock's film *Psycho*. According to Kristeva, the corpse is the most extreme example of the abject, because the entire body is turned into waste. As children, Liza and her brother Kenny play with the discarded innards, assuring their father that they themselves are safe from pollution: 'We wash our hands in Borax soap' (*OS* 286).

The corpse is in transition between life and death, subject and object. Taxidermy accentuates this ambiguity by reassembling the organic with the aid of the inorganic:

> Skin lay in piles, folded flesh-side out. Heads of animals, with empty eyeholes and mouth holes, were set on stands. What she thought at first was the skinned body of a deer turned out to be only a wire armature with bundles of what looked like glued straw tied to it. (*OS* 273)

Bea sees these apparently lifelike creatures are merely skins 'around a body in which nothing was real' (*OS* 287). Skin is a dangerously permeable border between the self and the exterior world. Munro describes Bea and Ladner lying together the night before his death, 'with all available bare skin touching – legs, arms, haunches' (*OS* 274), as the lovers try to merge with one another. Even as they try to transcend bodily limits, their corporeality is emphasized by the zoological 'haunches'. Ladner's scar, 'the splotch on his face that shone like metal in the sunlight coming through the trees' suggests a camouflaged animal.

94

Mimicking Bea for the benefit of the children, Liza and Kenny, as they all play in his pond, Ladner acts like a live bird:

His body was stiff but he turned his head sharply from side to side, skimming or patting the water with fluttery hands. Preening, twitching, as if carried away with admiration for himself. (*OS* 288)

However, when he makes a grab at Liza, his body collapses 'like the pelt of an animal flung loose from its flesh and bones'. His eyes are 'hard and round as the animals' glass eyes' (*OS* 292). When we gaze into someone's eyes, we are trying to glimpse their soul. At this moment, Ladner has none; he is himself a corpse.

Liza's memory of being molested by Ladner recapitulates the imagery associated with the attack on his exhibits. The glass eye recalls the 'bitter red eye' of a damaged bird, which is already linked to Ladner by Warren's words, 'Do you care if he croaks?' (*OS* 284). Liza's own birdlike croaks, as she touches 'her teeth, her pointed tongue to his neck' in response, mimics Ladner just as, later in the story, but chronologically earlier, Ladner mimics Bea.

'The traitor, the liar, the criminal with a good conscience, the shameless rapist, the killer who claims he is a saviour' is also abject.[3] Like these examples, Ladner appears contradictory and duplicitous, from Liza's perspective. 'He could switch from one person to another and make it your fault if you remembered' (*OS* 289). His behaviour is an unstoppable physical force like 'an invasion of pins and needles' (*OS* 290) – or like the delirious spasms that accompany abjection. This treacherous ambiguity reveals itself as much in his mimicry of Bea as it does in his behaviour towards Liza. Bea and Ladner are Liza's surrogate parents. Compounding what we may consider to be incestuous abuse, Ladner's mockery flouts maternal authority.

Liza is fascinated by his parodic display: 'Part of her wanted to make Ladner stop at once, before the damage was done, and part of her longed for that very damage, the damage Ladner could do, the ripping open, the final delight of it' (*OS* 288).

Bea could spread safety if she wanted to. Surely she could. All that is needed is for her to turn herself into a different sort of woman, a hard-and-fast, draw-the-line sort, clean-sweeping, energetic and intolerant. *None of that. Not allowed. Be good.* (*OS* 293)

Liza is forced to 'draw the line' herself, abjecting the mother and identifying with paternal law, in the form of puritanical Christianity.

Both 'parents', Bea and Ladner, are, in some respects, identified with the maternal, and both are abjected. For Liza, as for Bea, Ladner's territory is full of maternal connotations. Like the man himself, it is polymorphous, 'a world of different and distinct countries'. Light, sound and smells are constantly shifting. Landscape and body are fused in 'places where Liza thinks there is a bruise on the ground, a tickling and shame in the grass'. The shade under the grass, resembling 'a black pond' recalls Liza's dive under the deep water (*OS* 291).

Bea does take control when she sends Liza to college. But, far from reinforcing the maternal bond, her generosity expels Liza from the family triad. Liza's destruction of Ladner's house may be seen in simple terms as punishment for child abuse. Her revenge is also directed against the exclusive parental dyad, and it re-enacts maternal abjection. Liza experiences a *jouissance* comparable to that of 'the ripping open, the final delight of it', promised by Ladner's mimicry.

Like carnival ambivalence, abject writing offers a space in which all the rules are subverted and boundaries crossed. Identities are multiplied and fixed meanings dissolve. Munro has often said that writing began as a means of ordering experience. In her *Meanjin* interview, she says that as her work has developed she has realized that 'the questions we ask are far more intriguing than the answers we give or sometimes think we've discovered'. Even though Munro's fiction challenges existing power structures, particularly those regarding gender and class, her stories are never didactic. While some critics may discern a message against paedophilia in 'Vandals', it is not a polemic directed against Ladner. It would be a simpler, more comfortable story if it were, confirming our own sanctity, as readers who do not participate in horror. Munro has described how, like generations of teenage girls, she was entranced by *Wuthering Heights*, and by Heathcliff, its brooding, sadistic hero. In her own fiction, Munro exposes the extent to which women condone male transgression, often, as in 'The Love of a Good Woman', in order to exert maternal control. But for Enid, for Bea, and many other Munro women, there is a deeper motivation, buried in their own desires, the need to find through their men 'an insanity that could contain them'. Bea comments sarcastically on 'all the dreary romances – some brute gets the woman tingling and then it's goodbye to Mr. Fine-and-Decent' (*OS* 268). But she is being a little disingenuous when she claims that this scenario is not behind her own attraction to Ladner.

Romance, drink and literature provide an escape from the everyday into a heightened existence. They are all addictive. When Munro says 'There were stories in my community about women who had become readers, in the way that they might take up drinking',[4] she implies secret misbehaviour – private self-indulgence. Bea likes a tipple; in 'Carried Away', Louisa's tongue is loosened by drink. Men are expected to drink, as is made plain in 'Spaceships Have Landed' (*OS* 226–60). Their reading is also more easily integrated into their social role. In 'Carried Away', Jack borrows purposeful volumes by Chesterton and Russell, with titles like *What's Wrong with the World?* and *Bolshevism: Practice and Theory*. Ladner is another autodidact. When Bea sees his books on the shelves she visualizes 'his orderly solitude, his systematic reading and barren contentment' (*OS* 273). Although he is a loner, he acquires factual information through his solitary reading. This practical approach contrasts with female reading habits throughout *Open Secrets*. Reading, drinking and romance all induce altered states, accentuating physical sensations and suspending time through *jouissance*. To read Munro is to share in that *jouissance*, whether it is experienced as the sublime or the abject.

There has never been a writer who relished the diversity of language as much as Alice Munro. But in every story, finally, words fail. There is always something which has to be left out, and can only be approximated through imagery and paradox. 'Vandals' closes with 'darkness collecting, rising among the trees, like cold smoke coming off the snow' (*OS* 294). We are in the dark forest, that unfathomable place where the fairy tales begin, and where we can't help gazing down that deep maternal well.

Notes

INTRODUCTION

1. Harold Bloom, *The Western Canon* (London and New York: Harcourt, Brace and Company, 1994).
2. 'Alice's Wonderland': interview with Dinitia Smith, *Ottawa Citizen*, 21 December 1998.
3. Pleuke Boyce and Ron Smith, 'A National Treasure: Interview with Alice Munro', in *Meanjin*, 54:2 (University of Melbourne, 1995), 222–32. The interview explains the origins of three stories in *Open Secrets* – 'Carried Away, 'An Albanian Virgin' and 'A Real Life' – as sections of the same novel.
4. Thomas E. Tausky, 'Biocritical Essay', in *The Alice Munro Papers: First Accession*, ed. Apollonia Steele and Jean F. Tener (Calgary: University of Calgary Press, 1986), xi.
5. Frank O'Connor, *The Lonely Voice: A Study of the Short Story* (London: Macmillan, 1963).
6. Margaret Atwood, Introduction, *The Oxford Book of Canadian Short Stories in English*, selected by Margaret Atwood and Robert Weaver (Toronto, Oxford and New York: Oxford University Press, 1986), xv.
7. Quoted in an interview with Alice Munro by Jeanne McCulloch and Mona Simpson, *Paris Review*, 131 (Summer 1994), 229.

CHAPTER 1. LOOKING AT THE MOON: THE FEMALE ARTIST

1. Julia Kristeva, 'Women's Time', in *The Kristeva Reader*, ed. Toril Moi (Oxford: Blackwell, 1993), 187–213.
2. Sylvia Plath, *The Bell Jar* (London: Faber and Faber, 1980), 85.
3. Ibid., 84.

Notes

4. Simone de Beauvoir, *The Second Sex*, trans. H. M. Parshley (Harmondsworth: Penguin, 1974), 716.
5. Not included in British edition (London: Vintage, 1997).

CHAPTER 2. THE BIOGRAPHICAL BACKGROUND

1. Graeme Gibson, 'Alice Munro', in *Eleven Canadian Novelists* (Toronto: Anansi, 1973), 246.
2. James Agee and Walker Evans, *Let Us Now Praise Famous Men* (London: Violette Editions, 2001), 215.
3. Paul de Man, 'Autobiography as De-facement', *Modern Language Notes*, 94 (1979), 921.
4. Beverley Rasporich, *Dance of the Sexes: Art and Gender in the Fiction of Alice Munro* (Edmonton: University of Alberta Press, 1990); Catherine Sheldrick Ross, *Alice Munro: A Double Life* (Toronto: ECW Press, 1992).
5. Magdalene Redekop, *Mothers and Other Clowns: The Stories of Alice Munro* (London and New York: Routledge, 1990).
6. Nancy Choderow, *The Reproduction of Mothering: Psychoanalysis and the Sociology of Gender* (Berkeley, Los Angeles and London: University of California Press, 1978).
7. M. M. Bakhtin, 'Author and Hero in Aesthetic Activity', in *Art and Answerability: Early Philosophical Essays by M. M. Bakhtin*, ed. Michael Holquist and Vadim Liupanov, trans. Vadim Liupanov (Austin: University of Texas Press, 1990), 33.
8. See Antonio Damasio, *The Feeling of What Happens: Body, Emotion and the Making of Consciousness* (London: Vintage, 2000) on 'primary' and 'secondary' emotions.
9. Online interview with the *New Yorker*, < www.newyorker.com >, 12 February 2001.
10. Sheila Munro, *Lives of Mothers and Daughters:Growing Up with Alice Munro* (Toronto: McClelland and Stewart, 2001).
11. Raymond Carver, 'Fires', in *Fires: Essays, Poems, Stories* (London: Harvill, 1991), 33.
12. Harold Horwood, 'Interview with Alice Munro' in *The Art of Alice Munro: Saying the Unsayable*, ed. Judith Miller (Ontario: University of Waterloo Press, 1984), 123–35.

CHAPTER 3. EPIPHANIES AND INTUITIONS: THE SHORT-STORY GENRE

1. See Poe's 1842 review, 'Nathaniel Hawthorne', in *Tales, Poems and Essays* (London: Collins, 1969), 520.
2. Henri Bergson, *Matter and Memory*, trans. N. M. Paul and W. S. Palmer (New York: Zone Books, 1991), 73.
3. James Joyce, *Stephen Hero* (London: Jonathan Cape, 1969), 218.
4. Virginia Woolf, 'A Sketch of the Past', in *Moments of Being: Unpublished Autobiographical Writings*, ed. Jeanne Schulkind (London: Sussex University Press, 1976), 70.
5. Katherine Mansfield, 'Bliss', in *The Collected Short Stories* (Harmondsworth: Penguin, 1984), 105.

CHAPTER 4. DID YOU TELL? SPEECH, SILENCE AND DOUBLE-VOICED DISCOURSE

1. Bakhtin, 'Discourse in the Novel', in *The Dialogic Imagination*, 333. Bakhtin refers to 'quasi-direct speech'. I use the term 'free indirect discourse' as the more common usage.
2. Cora Kaplan, 'Language and Gender' in *The Feminist Critique of Language: A Reader*, ed. Deborah Cameron (London: Routledge, 1995), 57–69.
3. Constance Rooke, 'Fear of the Open Heart', in *A Mazing Space: Writing Canadian Women Writing*, ed. Shirley Neuman and Smaro Kamboureli (Edmonton, Albert: Longspoon Press, 1986), 23.
4. Kaplan, 'Language and Gender', 66.
5. Magdalene Redekop, *Mothers and Other Clowns: The Stories of Alice Munro* (London and New York: Routledge, 1992), 22.
6. Grace Paley, 'A Conversation with my Father', in *Enormous Changes at the Last Minute* (London: Virago, 1990).
7. It may, or may not, be coincidental that Mrs Quinn shares her surname with Munro's editor, and that she dies on Munro's birthday. Perhaps these interconnections are best understood as more jokes and riddles without solutions.
8. Carol L. Beran, 'The Luxury of Excellence: Alice Munro in the *New Yorker*', in *Essays on Canadian Writing*, 66 (1998), 204–30.

CHAPTER 5. TURNING POINTS

1. James Agee and Walker Evans, *Let Us Now Praise Famous Men* (London: Violette Editions, 2001), 215.
2. M. M. Bakhtin, *Problems of Dostoevsky's Poetics*, ed. and trans. by Caryl Emerson (Manchester: Manchester University Press, 1984), 6.
3. See Carol L. Beran, 'The Luxury of Excellence: Alice Munro in the *New Yorker*', in *Essays on Canadian Writing*, 66 (1998), 204–30.
4. Linda Hutcheon, *A Poetics of Postmodernism* (London: Routledge, 1988), x.
5. Carol L. Beran, 'Thomas Hardy, Alice Munro and the Question of Influence', in the *American Review of Canadian Studies*, 29:2 (Summer 1999), 237–58.

CHAPTER 6. RECONSTRUCTING THE PAST

1. Henri Bergson, *Matter and Memory*, trans. N. M. Paul and W. S. Palmer (New York: Zone Books, 1996), 150.
2. M. M. Bakhtin, 'Author and Hero in Aesthetic Activity', in *Art and Answerability*, ed. Michael Holquist and Vadim Liapunov, trans. Vadim Liapunov (Austin: University of Texas Press, 1996), 23.
3. Alice Munro, 'The Colonel's Hash Resettled', in *How Stories Mean*, ed. John Metcalf and J. R. (Tim) Struthers (Ontario: Porcupine's Quill, 1973), 189.
4. 'It may be a way of getting on top of experience; this is different from one's experience of the things in the world, the experience with other people and with oneself, which can be so confusing and humiliating and difficult ... I think it's a way of getting control' (Graeme Gibson, 'Alice Munro', in *Eleven Canadian Novelists* (Toronto: Anansi, 1973), 245).
5. M. M. Bakhtin, 'Forms of Time and of the Chronotope in the Novel', in *The Dialogic Imagination*, ed. Michael Holquist, trans. Caryl Emerson and Michael Holquist (Austin: University of Texas Press, 1992), 247–8.
6. Interview with Lorrie Moore, *Paris Review*, 158 (2001), 72.
7. Robert Thacker, 'Introduction: Alice Munro, Writing "Home": "Seeing This Trickle in Time" ', *Essays in Canadian Writing*, 66 (1998), 1–20.

CHAPTER 7. AGEING, DECAY, ABJECTION

1. Julia Kristeva, *Desire in Language: A Semiotic Approach to Literature and Art*, ed. Léon S. Roudiez, trans. Thomas Gora, Alice Jardine and Léon S. Roudiez (Oxford: Blackwell, 1980), 283.
2. Julia Kristeva, *Powers of Horror: An Essay on Abjection*, trans. Léon S. Roudiez (New York : Columbia University Press, 1982), 6.
3. Kristeva, *Powers of Horror*, 4.
4. Eleanor Wachtel, 'Interview with Alice Munro', *Brick*, 40 (Winter 1991), 49–53.

Select Bibliography

WORKS BY ALICE MUNRO

Fiction

Dance of the Happy Shades (1968; London: Vintage, 2000). Contains: 'Walker Brothers Cowboy'; 'The Shining Houses'; 'Images'; 'Thanks for the Ride'; 'The Office'; 'An Ounce of Cure'; 'The Time of Death'; 'Day of the Butterfly'; 'Boys and Girls'; 'Postcard'; 'Red Dress – 1946'; 'Sunday Afternoon'; 'A Trip to the Coast'; 'The Peace of Utrecht'; 'Dance of the Happy Shades'.

Lives of Girls and Women (1971; Harmondsworth: Penguin, 1984). Contains: 'The Flats Road'; 'Heirs of the Living Body'; 'Princess Ida'; 'Age of Faith'; 'Changes and Ceremonies'; 'Lives of Girls and Women'; 'Baptizing'; 'Epilogue: The Photographer'.

Something I've Been Meaning to Tell You (1974; Harmondsworth: Penguin, 1987). Contains: 'Something I've Been Meaning to Tell You'; 'Material'; 'How I Met My Husband'; 'Walking on Water'; 'Forgiveness in Families'; 'Tell Me Yes or No'; 'The Found Boat'; 'Executioners'; 'Marrakesh'; 'The Spanish Lady'; 'Winter Wind'; 'Memorial'; 'The Ottawa Valley'.

The Beggar Maid, published in Canada under the title *Who Do You Think You Are?* (1978; Harmondsworth: Penguin, 1988). Contains: 'Royal Beatings'; 'Privilege'; 'Half a Grapefruit'; 'Wild Swans'; 'The Beggar Maid'; 'Mischief'; 'Providence'; 'Simon's Luck'; 'Spelling'; 'Who Do You Think You Are?'.

The Moons of Jupiter (1982; London: Vintage, 1997). Contains: 'Chaddeleys and Flemings: I "Connection", II "The Stone in the Field" '; 'Dulse'; 'The Turkey Season'; 'Accident'; 'Bardon Bus'; 'Prue'; 'Labor Dinner'; 'Mrs Cross and Mrs Kidd'; 'Hard-Luck Stories'; 'Visitors'; 'The Moons of Jupiter'.

The Progress of Love (1986; London: Flamingo, 1988). Contains: 'The Progress of Love'; 'Lichen'; 'Monsieur les Deux Chapeaux'; 'Miles

105

City, Montana'; 'Fits'; 'The Moon in the Orange Street Rink'; 'Jesse and Meribeth'; 'Eskimo'; 'A Queer Streak'; 'C Prayer'; 'White Dump'.

Friend of My Youth (1990; London: Vintage, 1991). Contains: 'Frier My Youth'; 'Five Points'; 'Meneseteung'; 'Hold Me Fast, Don't Me Pass'; 'Oranges and Apples'; 'Picture of the Ice'; 'Goodness a Mercy'; 'Oh, What Avails'; 'Differently'; 'Wigtime'.

Open Secrets (1994; London: Vintage, 1995). Contains: 'Carried Away' 'A Real Life'; 'The Albanian Virgin'; 'Open Secrets'; 'The Jack Randa Hotel'; 'A Wilderness Station'; 'Spaceships Have Landed'; 'Vandals'.

The Love of a Good Woman (1998; London: Vintage, 2000). Contains: 'The Love of a Good Woman'; 'Jakarta'; 'Cortes Island'; 'Save the Reaper'; 'The Children Stay'; 'Rich as Stink'; 'Before the Change'; 'My Mother's Dream'.

Hateship, Friendship, Courtship, Loveship, Marriage (London: Chatto & Windus, 2001). Contains: 'Hateship, Friendship, Courtship, Loveship, Marriage'; 'Floating Bridge'; 'Family Furnishings'; 'Com- fort'; 'Nettles'; 'Post and Beam'; 'What Is Remembered'; 'Queenie'; 'The Bear Came Over the Mountain'.

Selected Stories (1996; London: Vintage, 1997).

Articles and Criticism

'The Colonel's Hash Resettled', in *The Narrative Voice: Short Stories and Reflections by Canadian Authors*, ed. J. Metcalf (Toronto: McGraw-Hill Ryerson, 1972).

'Everything Here is Touchable and Mysterious', *Weekend Magazine, Toronto Star*, 5 November 1974.

'What is Real?', in *How Stories Mean*, ed. J. Metcalf and J. R. (Tim) Struthers (Erin, Ontario: Porcupine's Quill, 1993), 331–4.

'What Do You Want to Know For?', in *Writing Away: The PEN Canada Travel Anthology*, ed. Constance Rooke (Toronto: McClelland and Stewart, 1994), 203–20.

The University of Calgary holds an Alice Munro archive. *The Alice Munro Papers: First and Second Accession*, ed. Apollonia Steele and an F. Tener (Calgary: University of Calgary Press, 1986, 1987) ails its contents.

ISM, INTERVIEWS AND BIOGRAPHY

nount of material, both in books and journal articles, is ced on Munro in Canada. This selection consists of titles sily available or have been especially useful in this study.

Essays in Canadian Writing, 66 (1998), *Alice Munro Writing On*, is a special edition on Munro, edited by Robert Thacker. It is essential reading for anyone interested in recent Munro criticism.

Beran, Carol L., 'Thomas Hardy, Alice Munro and the Question of Influence', in the *American Review of Canadian Studies*, 29:2 (Summer 1999), 237–58.

Boyce, Pleuke, and Ron Smith, 'A National Treasure: Interview with Alice Munro', *Meanjin*, 54:2 (University of Melbourne, 1995), 222–32.

Carrington, Ildiko de Papp, *Controlling the Uncontrollable: The Fiction of Alice Munro* (Dekalb, IL: Northern Illinois University Press, 1989).

——'What's in a Title? Alice Munro's "Carried Away" ', *Sudies in Short Fiction*, 30:4 (1993), 55–64.

Carscallen, James, *The Other Country: Patterns in the Writing of Alice Munro* (Ontario: ECW Press, 1993).

Clark, Miriam Marty, 'Allegories of Reading in Alice Munro's "Carried Away" ', *Contemporary Literature*, 37:1 (1996), 49–62.

Gibson, Graeme, *Eleven Canadian Novelists* (Toronto: Anansi, 1973).

Hancock, Geoff, *Canadian Writers at Work: Interviews with Geoff Hancock* (Toronto: Oxford University Press, 1987).

Heble, Ajay, *The Tumble of Reason: Alice Munro's Discourse of Absence* (Toronto: University of Toronto Press, 1994).

Howells, Coral Ann, *Alice Munro* (Manchester: Manchester University Press, 1998).

Lecker, Robert, and Jack David, *Annotated Bibliography of Canada's Major Authors: Morley Callaghan, Mavis Gallant, Hugh Wood, Alice Munro, Ethel Wilson* (Toronto: ECW Press, 1994).

MacKendrick, Louis (ed.), *Probable Fictions: Alice Munro's Narrative Acts* (Toronto: ECW Press, 1983).

McCulloch, Jeanne, and Mona Simpson, 'Interview with Alice Munro', *Paris Review*, 131 (Summer 1994), 227–64.

Martin, W. R., *Alice Munro: Paradox and Parallel* (Edmonton: University of Alberta Press).

Mayberry, Katherine J., 'Every Last Thing . . . Everlasting: Alice Munro and the Limits of Narrative', *Studies in Short Fiction*, 29:4 (1992), 531–41.

Miller, Judith (ed.), *The Art of Alice Munro: Saying the Unsayable* (Waterloo, Ontario: University of Waterloo Press, 1984).

Munro, Sheila, *Lives of Mothers and Daughters: Growing Up with Alice Munro* (Toronto: McClelland and Stewart, 2001).

Neuman, Shirley, and Smaro Kamboureli (eds.), *A Mazing Space: Writing Canadian Women Writing* (Edmonton, Alberta: Longspoon Press, 1986).

107

Osmond, Rosalie, 'Arrangements, "Disarrangements" and "Earnest Deceptions" ', in *Narrative Strategies*, ed. Coral A. Howells and Lynette Hunter (Milton Keynes: Open University Press, 1991), 82–92.

Rasporich, Beverley J., *Dance of the Sexes: Art and Gender in the Fiction of Alice Munro* (Edmonton: University of Alberta Press, 1990).

Redekop, Magdalene, *Mothers and Other Clowns: The Stories of Alice Munro* (London and New York: Routledge, 1992).

Ross, Catherine Sheldrick, *Alice Munro: A Double Life* (Toronto: ECW Press, 1992).

——'Interview with Alice Munro', *Canadian Children's Literature*, 53 (1989), 14–24.

Smith, Dinitia, 'Alice's Wonderland', *Ottawa Citizen*, 21 December 1998.

Tausky, Thomas E., 'Biocritical Essay', in *The Alice Munro Papers: First Accession*, ed. Apollonia Steele and Jean F. Tener (Calgary: University of Calgary Press, 1986), ix–xxiv.

Thacker, Robert, ' "Go Ask Alice": The Progress of Munro Criticism', *Journal of Canadian Studies*, 26:2 (1991), 156–69.

——'What's "Material"? The Progress of Munro Criticism, Part 2', *Journal of Canadian Studies*, 33:2 (1998).

Wachtel, Eleanor, 'Interview with Alice Munro', *Brick*, 40 (1991), 49–53.

BACKGROUND READING

Agee, James, and Walker Evans, *Let Us Now Praise Famous Men* (London: Violette Editions, 2001).

Bakhtin, M. M., *Art and Answerability: Early Philosophical Essays by M. M. Bakhtin*, ed. Michael Holquist and Vadim Liupanov, trans. Vadim Liupanov (Austin: University of Texas Press, 1990).

——*The Dialogic Imagination: Four Essays by M. M. Bakhtin*, ed. Michael Holquist, trans. Caryl Emerson and Michael Holquist (Austin: University of Texas Press, 1992).

——*Problems of Dostoevsky's Poetics*, ed. and trans. Caryl Emerson (Manchester: Manchester University Press, 1984).

——*Rabelais and His World*, trans. H. Iswolsky (Bloomington: Indiana University Press, 1984).

——*Speech Genres and Other Late Essays*, ed. Caryl Emerson and Michael Holquist, trans. Vern W. McGee (Austin: University of Texas Press, 1992).

Beauvoir, Simone de, *The Second Sex*, trans. H. M. Parshley (Harmondsworth: Penguin, 1974).

Bergson, Henri, *Matter and Memory*, trans. N. M. Paul and W. S. Palmer (New York: Zone Books, 1996).

Bloom, Harold, *The Western Canon* (London and New York: Harcourt, Brace and Company, 1994).

Carver, Raymond, *Fires: Essays, Poems, Stories* (London: Harvill, 1991).

Choderow, Nancy, *The Reproduction of Mothering: Psychoanalysis and the Sociology of Gender* (Berkeley, Los Angeles and London: University of California Press, 1978).

Damasio, Antonio, *The Feeling of What Happens: Body, Emotion and the Making of Consciousness* (London: Vintage, 2000).

Hutcheon, Linda, *A Poetics of Postmodernism* (London: Routledge, 1988).

Joyce, James, *Stephen Hero* (London: Jonathan Cape, 1969).

Kaplan, Cora, 'Language and Gender', in *The Feminist Critique of Language: A Reader*, ed. Deborah Cameron (London: Routledge, 1995), 57–69.

Kristeva, Julia, *Desire in Language: A Semiotic Approach to Literature and Art*, ed. Léon S. Roudiez, trans. Thomas Gora, Alice Jardine and Léon S. Roudiez (Oxford: Blackwell, 1980).

——Powers of Horror: An Essay on Abjection, trans. Léon S. Roudiez (New York: Columbia University Press, 1982).

——'Women's Time', trans. Alice Jardine and Harry Blake, in *The Kristeva Reader*, ed. Toril Moi (Oxford: Blackwell, 1993), 187–213.

Man, Paul de, 'Autobiography as De-facement', *Modern Language Notes*, 94 (1979), 931–55.

Mansfield, Katherine, *The Collected Short Stories* (Harmondsworth: Penguin, 1984).

Plath, Sylvia, *The Bell Jar* (London: Faber and Faber, 1980).

Poe, Edgar Allan, 'Nathaniel Hawthorne', *Tales, Poems and Essays* (London: Collins, 1969), 513–25.

Woolf, Virginia, *Moments of Being: Unpublished Autobiographical Writings*, ed. Jeanne Schulkind (London: Sussex University Press, 1976).

Index

Recent and Forthcoming Titles in the New Series of

WRITERS AND THEIR WORK

"... this series promises to outshine its own previously high reputation."
Times Higher Education Supplement

"...will build into a fine multi-volume critical encyclopaedia of English literature."
Library Review & Reference Review

"...Excellent, informative, readable, and recommended."
NATE News

"written by outstanding contemporary critics, whose expertise is flavoured by unashamed enthusiasm for their subjects and the series' diverse aspirations."
Times Educational Supplement

"A useful and timely addition to the ranks of the lit crit and reviews genre. Written in an accessible and authoritative style."
Library Association Record

WRITERS AND THEIR WORK

RECENT & FORTHCOMING TITLES

Title	Author
William Hazlitt	J. B. Priestley; R. L. Brett (intro. by Michael Foot)
Seamus Heaney 2/e	Andrew Murphy
George Herbert	T.S. Eliot (intro. by Peter Porter)
Geoffrey Hill	Andrew Roberts
Gerard Manley Hopkins	Daniel Brown
Henrik Ibsen	Sally Ledger
Kazuo Ishiguro	Cynthia Wong
Henry James – The Later Writing	Barbara Hardy
James Joyce	Steven Connor
Julius Caesar	Mary Hamer
Franz Kafka	Michael Wood
John Keats	Kelvin Everest
Hanif Kureishi	Ruvani Ranasinha
William Langland: Piers Plowman	Claire Marshall
King Lear	Terence Hawkes
Philip Larkin	Laurence Lerner
D. H. Lawrence	Linda Ruth Williams
Doris Lessing	Elizabeth Maslen
C. S. Lewis	William Gray
Wyndham Lewis	Andrzej Gasiorak
David Lodge	Bernard Bergonzi
Katherine Mansfield	Andrew Bennett
Christopher Marlowe	Thomas Healy
Andrew Marvell	Annabel Patterson
Ian McEwan	Kiernan Ryan
Measure for Measure	Kate Chedgzoy
A Midsummer Night's Dream	Helen Hackett
Alice Munro	Ailsa Cox
Vladimir Nabokov	Neil Cornwell
V. S. Naipaul	Suman Gupta
Edna O'Brien	Amanda Greenwood
Ben Okri	Robert Fraser
Walter Pater	Laurel Brake
Brian Patten	Linda Cookson
Harold Pinter	Mark Batty
Sylvia Plath 2/e	Elisabeth Bronfen
Jean Rhys	Helen Carr
Richard II	Margaret Healy
Richard III	Edward Burns
Dorothy Richardson	Carol Watts
John Wilmot, Earl of Rochester	Germaine Greer
Romeo and Juliet	Sasha Roberts
Christina Rossetti	Kathryn Burlinson
Salman Rushdie	Damian Grant
Paul Scott	Jacqueline Banerjee
The Sensation Novel	Lyn Pykett
P. B. Shelley	Paul Hamilton
Wole Soyinka	Mpalive Msiska
Muriel Spark	Brian Cheyette
Edmund Spenser	Colin Burrow
Laurence Sterne	Manfred Pfister
D. M. Thomas	Bran Nicol
Dylan Thomas	Chris Wiggington

RECENT & FORTHCOMING TITLES

Title	Author
J. R. R. Tolkien	*Charles Moseley*
Leo Tolstoy	*John Bayley*
Charles Tomlinson	*Tim Clark*
Anthony Trollope	*Andrew Sanders*
Victorian Quest Romance	*Robert Fraser*
Edith Wharton	*Janet Beer*
Angus Wilson	*Peter Conradi*
Mary Wollstonecraft	*Jane Moore*
Women's Gothic 2/e	*Emma Clery*
Virginia Woolf 2/e	*Laura Marcus*
Working Class Fiction	*Ian Haywood*
W. B. Yeats	*Edward Larrissy*
Charlotte Yonge	*Alethea Hayter*

Printed and bound by CPI Group (UK) Ltd, Croydon, CR0 4YY

09/06/2025

14685822-0002